F.Y.I.

© 2019 Simply LaChish. All rights reserved. No part of this publication may be reproduced, stored in a retrieval system, or transmitted in any form by any way means electronic, mechanical, photocopying, recording or otherwise without permission of the author.

For more information contact: www.SimplyLaChish.com

Library of Congress Control Number: 1-8126969521
Printed in the United States
Published by: ITMM/KDP
Edited By: Kingdom Publishing

F.Y.I.
Freeing Yourself Indefinitely
By Simply LaChish

𝓕. 𝒴. 𝐼.

Table of Contents

i. Dedication 4
ii. Acknowledgments 5
iii. Pre- Journey Instructions 6
iv. Foreword 8
1. Naked and Unashamed 10
2. Perfection Almost Killed Me 23
3. The Blame Game: It's GOD's Fault 37
4. The Thoughtless Prayer Request 47
5. Demonstrators Post: Know Your Role 60
6. Silent Scream: Unleash Your Voice 74
7. During the Pain 90
8. Free Yourself 114
9. Do the Root Work 146
10. Free Indeed 165

References 177

F. Y. I.

F.Y.I. is dedicated to

Dr. Mack LaKendrick Knight

Affectionately known as "Kenny"

May your life and legacy live on forever; your impact on my life absolutely will. You mastered the freedom to enter eternity with a courage and dignity I still struggle to accept. Thank you for being a genuine, gentle, and GIANT spirit on this earth. We miss you.

"A mind that has been stretched cannot return to its original dimension." Dr. Kenny Knight

F. Y. I.

Acknowledgments

I honor my children: Destiny, Daniel Jr, Judah, Zion, and Izreal for blessing me with your presence, love, inspiration, and motivation to be my best self.

I honor my family and friends who relentlessly support and encourage me in every season of my life. I am grateful for each of you, far too many to name. I want to give a special shout out to Edwina Braswell and Tracie Stanley who encouraged me to complete this project and held me accountable along my journey.

I want to acknowledge my production team: Photo credit: Stylist Sammie Haynes www.sammihaynes.com, Photographer Blair Devereaux www.pheauxtography.com, Hairstylists Lakisha 'Karizzma' Beauford @itskarizzma, Make-Up Artists Shaneka Murray @sunshani_mua. Cover Design: Izii Designer. Editors: Professor Mary Mocsary and Pastor Martina L. Mitchell. Publishing: In Touch with Martina Mitchell.

I want to thank my mentor of nearly twenty years, Evangelist Faye Dadzie for the foreword. I thank GOD for placing such a powerful, consistent, loving, wise, and humble woman in my life to help me navigate from being a broken teenager to a wise, whole woman.

Thank you to each person who has taken the time to purchase this project. You are helping me fulfill my passion for funding scholarships for higher education. You are the true MVP!

F. Y. I.

Pre-Journey Instructions

Dear Friend, I am so elated about this opportunity to share some very personal and powerful information I have learned. This has been the hardest book for me to write. In times past, I have written each book after a great storm or enlightening event. This book has taken me years to complete versus the month, or so my former books took. I began writing this book years ago and stopped multiple times along the way. I kept getting sidetracked because I was not quite ready to be completely honest with my process. I couldn't write about being free when I was still worried about how others would interpret or critique my content. I wrestled with the most politically correct way to present my journey. I hit brick walls every time I tried to limit, censor, or color the portrait in any way that was not authentic to the raw experience I was enduring. I'm proud to say, once I overcame that chain, I was able to write the most powerful message I have shared to this point in my life.

I want to prepare you for a transparent journey of the emotional, mental, and spiritual resolve of a conqueror with universal principles that you can apply to your life. This is a journey through captivity to restore liberty. We are dismantling the strongholds in your mind and breaking lifelong chains one link at a time. I will share with you my complete process from the prison to the place of victory and liberty I possess today. Prepare to stop sabotaging yourself and walk-in total liberty, by dismantling self-sabotaging thoughts and correcting your vision of life. You will begin building the toolbox to navigate your life

F. Y. I.

successfully, learning to find wisdom in everything you experience. You will reclaim mental clarity, liberty, and authority.

When existing is not enough, break free from captivity and live! You are worth it! You deserve the abundant life you were promised. Many say life is what you make it. I believe life is what you think it to be. Brace yourself for the journey. There will be highs. There may be lows. There will be moments when you are face to face with emotions you have avoided for many years. Fear not! At the end of this therapeutic journey, you will never be the same. If you open your heart and mind to receive the principles offered in this book, I guarantee you will be fully capable of Freeing Yourself Indefinitely! I'm so confident that I will give your money back if you don't.

I'm excited for your Freedom Journey. Please use the companion workbook as you read. It will reinforce the principles with opportunities to apply to your personal life experiences.

Let's get started! I'll see you on the free side!

Humbly,

Simply LaChish

F. Y. I.

Foreword

Evangelist Faye Dadzie

    Almost 20 years ago, while preaching for a women's retreat, I met a tiny, soft-spoken, teenaged girl. She was there in the midst of a group of women where anyone could have been her mother or grandmother. She was very humble and unobtrusive but had a presence even then that was unique yet engaging. I ministered the Word, and she ministered powerfully through dance. Even though her physical stature gave the appearance of fragility, as I observed her and talked with her, there was a latent determination and grit that gave a sneak peek into who this girl would become. She had questions about many things, and though she was shy and apologetic about "taking up my time," she took every minute that she asked for and engaged me in heartfelt, thought-provoking, and transparent conversation.

    Over the years as she has transitioned from girl to woman. God has done marvelous things in her life. Lest I mislead you, that previous statement by no stretch of the imagination is intended to portray a Cinderella fairy tale. Like all of us, life has happened to her! She became a wife, mother, military officer, medical professional, preacher, Co-Pastor, mentor, and friend to many philanthropist, and most of all a full-fledged, legitimate giant in the Kingdom of God. That glimpse of the guts and grace that were housed in that tiny frame all those years ago has exploded on the scene to the glory of God and for all to see. It is her steadfast, unwavering commitment to the cause of Christ that has built her up. It has propped her up and still lifts her

F. Y. I.

above the fray, the foolishness, and ultimately the failure that the enemy would desire.

Freeing Yourself Indefinitely (F.Y.I.) gives you a front-row seat to observe, but more importantly, to experience the realness of this faith walk. It is not always pretty and comforting, but rather exposes the hard places that many of us have faced, but lacked the courage or conviction to confront head-on. Life on the front line includes becoming a target and sometimes getting wounded. It incurs the difficult and arduous task of healing. But it also teaches us strategies that are critically necessary to survive and thrive.

If you are tired of the pain and you are ready to become the best version of yourself, rest here. If you are no longer willing to be manipulated by relationships and your own emotions, come on and participate in the gleaning and growing that is available in Freeing Yourself Indefinitely. This "tiny giant" has used her strength to kick the door down. Now you can walk in.

Evangelist Faye Dadzie

Founder of Victorious Life Ministries

www.vl-ministries.org

Chapter One

Naked and Unashamed

I am writing you this very personal letter because I have found myself trapped in a place far too long and am trying to figure out how to break free. I have lost my footing. I have lost my direction. I have lost my bearings. I have lost my hope. I have lost my faith. I have lost my belief that certain situations I have faced for years will ever change. I have lost my concern with how you will judge my words. I have lost my desire to use my words to speak. Yes, I have restricted myself from standing before people and speaking for the last three+ years of my life because I lost my desire to be a voice. I stopped counseling people. I stopped coaching people. I stopped mentoring people. I stopped helping other people. I was tired of pouring out, but not having a consistent source to pour into me. I am tired of being the bigger person. I am tired of being the one obligated to do the "right" thing, even though wrong, was done to me repeatedly and with no regard for my sanity, my heart, or my humanity. I am in fact, more than tired. I am EXHAUSTED, and now, I am over "it!"

If you're uncomfortable with that first paragraph, this book may be difficult for you to read. As I write, I have given myself permission to get naked. Knowing how I am, getting naked is extremely uncomfortable because I do not mind showing skin, but I have parts of my body I just don't feel comfortable exposing. I cannot see myself standing naked before a crowd of people, or posing naked for a

F. Y. I.

photoshoot, or being completely naked in a locker room, changing in front of other women. I can tolerate going down to my two-piece swimsuit, but the private parts have to remain covered. Why am I saying this? The same way I am uncomfortable getting completely naked physically in front of others, I am even more uncomfortable being completely naked emotionally and mentally to people. I never know who's going to judge me. I know I will be judged, but how will I be judged is the uncertain part.

When you've acquired respect and admiration from people, who see you fully clothed…let me make this more personal…When I have acquired "respect" and "admiration" from people who see me fully clothed, fully dressed, fully put together, fully functional, getting naked in front of them makes me uncertain that their same enthusiasm for my clothed image will continue with my naked self. It's such a common uncertainty I see in our society. When a woman is dressed up, and her makeup artist has made her face perfect, and her hairstylist has made her hair beautiful, and she appears flawless, this woman is adored by men and women. She is attractive. She is used as a gauge or standard that other women are mentally compared with to define their level of beauty and/or attractiveness. However, that same woman can be found on vacation at a beach with no hair and makeup artist, and her natural features can be ostracized for not being as beautiful as her "put together" image portrays. Tabloid magazines will even make this image a cover photo to catch your eye while checking out of the store. Then there are statements made, such as "she's pretty with makeup."

I think this is one reason I never really learned how to apply makeup to myself. I am not even good at purchasing makeup. I have nothing against it or people who

F. Y. I.

wear it faithfully. I actually enjoy it when someone else does it for me, and the enhancements it makes to my appearance. Nevertheless, there is one problem I have with makeup, it amplifies my blemishes. When I wear makeup, and my concealer and foundation are perfectly blended, my skin is evened and toned. My bone structure is highlighted beautifully. I see the "perfected" image of my face. I see what my face would look like if I didn't have dark rings under my eyes, freckles forming on my cheekbones, marks or scars on my face or uneven toning from sun exposure. I'm guilty of not washing my face for a day after a photoshoot because I like the way the makeup artist applied certain cosmetics I do not know how to replicate. I am forced to admit an insecurity that my bear naked face is not as beautiful as my painted face. I have to become comfortable with my blemishes when the concealer and foundation are washed away. Therefore, if I feel this way with makeup, you can imagine the challenge I feel with removing the concealer from my soul and bearing my naked self in an age of judgment and false pretense.

    I am brave, though. I am willing to expose myself ONLY because I know there are others who are waiting for permission to be naked as well. I have never been to a nude beach, but I imagine part of the courage given to first-timers is knowing that they will be surrounded by others who are just as exposed as they are. If someone decides to stare, evaluate, or assess their body, they have full liberty to stare back, evaluate, and assess too. It's fair. Everyone is equally at risk. Therefore, everyone is conscious not to be too hard in their judgments.

    Being naked should not bring anxiety or discomfort. It is natural. It is how we enter this world, but isn't it funny that it is not how we leave it? Some people are dressed nicer in their caskets than they are the whole time they

F. Y. I.

lived. Some people's first time wearing eye-shadow and blush is in the casket, so the people viewing their bodies for the last time see the deceased in a way that is not startling, or too revealing of their real condition. In addition, the family can be proud of how they laid their loved ones to rest. And the family can display their affection for their loved ones with dignity. It is expected.

Adam and Eve were comfortable being naked physically until they became uncomfortable being naked emotionally. They began hiding everything, trying to hide one thing [1].

When they began to feel ashamed for making a bad decision, they wanted to cover up their emotions and their bodies. They tried to cover their new truth. Their mistake caused their personal vision to change. Suddenly, they were naked. Actually they were always naked. Adam and Eve were comfortable being naked as long as they were comfortable telling the truth. Once they were uncomfortable telling GOD the truth, they became uncomfortable being seen naked. Honestly, they are not the only ones who have resorted to hiding multiple things, trying to hide one area of shame.

Where can you be completely naked and comfortable? I've watched people work hard to hide their wounds. In trying to hide one thing, they created a myriad of outward distractions to conceal an inward disaster. You have seen it yourself in misbehaving children. By the time you sit down and get to the root of what seemed to be a behavioral problem, you discover it was really an emotional secret that tormented them. I have been there myself, expressing anger to avoid revealing brokenness. This is the society we live in, where a man crying out on social media about his heart being broken turns into an opportunity for others to laugh, belittle, ostracize, and criticize. He was rejected because he was too honest. How does that even make sense? Perhaps, that's where the term "brutally honest" came originated. Sharing a level of truth and honesty that people do not want to hear, or are not familiar with hearing, or are not comfortable with hearing is being brutally honest. It seems we should call our society brutally DIS-honest.

We have become accepting of telling selective truths, convenient truths, comfortable truths, complimentary truths, truths that make us feel good. We are resistant, reluctant, and sometimes, turned off by raw unfiltered truth. We laugh at the famous movie quote "You can't handle the truth![2]", as if it is not our reality. Many of us live from day to day, afraid of finding out the real truth, the full truth, the unfiltered truth. We have become weakened by the continuous charade of dishonesty, partial truths, and fabricated statements that we are often emotionally unprepared to hear. What has become "normal" is dysfunctional and not the healthy norm we need to surpass surviving life to living it.

I have always been a person to say I would rather be told the truth, regardless of how hurtful it is. I am still that person, but I have learned the truth can be more devastating than we can prepare for mentally. I found out something about myself while enduring a series of truths delivered to me. For one, I could handle the information, but I could not always handle the person bringing the information. Second, I could handle the information, but I was turned off by the motive of the person delivering it. Should these things have mattered?

F. Y. I.

I could not understand why this mattered until I realized some people were using the truth as a weapon. Their motives and intentions were to damage me, to hurt me, or to make me feel the hurt they were experiencing alone. Some of their motives were to hurt others connected to me. For that reason, they used me as collateral damage to hurt the person to whom they no longer had direct access since they knew I did. Some people were angry with one person and wanted me to be angry with that individual as well. Some people were trying to help and protect me. No matter what they were trying to accomplish, I had to decide what I would do with the truth.

It is easy to reject a truth you don't want to hear.

I can admit in some situations, I struggled to decipher the truth from falsehood with a few extra ingredients of truth mixed in. I wanted the truth detached from the talebearer's emotional investments, but I got the truth based on their emotional incitements.

How could spreading the truth be damaging? Why would I care if people knew the truth unless I was concerned that truth would damage the lie? Why would I want a lie to prevail more than the truth? I wouldn't. Right? Did I want a lie to prevail? No, I did not want a lie to prevail. I wanted to tell my truth myself!

Because GOD didn't make me afraid of truth-telling, admitting my fumbles, stumbles, and bad choices are effortless. I am the wrong person to try to blackmail because I will admit my mistakes before allowing anyone to use my actions against me. I have no qualms taking

F. Y. I.

responsibility for myself. I wish everyone around me were the same way, but I am keenly aware this is not the case.

Everyone should be careful with whom you share sensitive information with. I have been warned many times, not every individual can handle someone else's transparency. But why do I have to be careful when I tell the truth? And what negative outcome should I fear if I tell the truth and someone repeats it? I should not fear the truth spreading; it's the lies I could fear spreading like wildfire. Though asinine, this is how we learn to live.

We are afraid to tell the truth. I venture to say we are terrified at times!

Medical appointments are great examples of times where telling the truth can be terrifying. As a nurse, I have screened patients that come in for doctors' appointments. I have to ask questions that are sensitive for some people. I need to ask how many drinks they have a month, week, or day. Sometimes, people lie to me because they know if their honest answer reveals more drinks than recommended, I have to ask additional questions, and that could lead to more evaluations. To avoid the inconvenience and prevent the label of being an alcoholic they would rather tell me a lie. I've done this long enough to identify when a patient is lying.

I have lied in medical appointments or counseling sessions when the medical staff asked questions to evaluate depression levels, suicide, or homicide risk levels. One of the first points the counselor makes, "There are some things I have to report if they are shared here." That prevents many people from being honest about those reportable

F. Y. I.

issues because they may not want to be admitted to inpatient mental health facilities, or get arrested, or be restrained.

Consider how honestly you would respond to the following screening questions if the answer to any were yes. Is there anyone you think about punching in the face? Do you ever have thoughts of doing bodily harm to someone? The initial response to any of these questions would be no. Yet, if I can be honest, there were times in my life where I have been frustrated enough to think about engaging in physical altercations. Just because I've had those isolated thoughts, does not mean I have acted in that manner. I have rarely allowed the thought to become an action. Yes, there were times when I actually fought people. I have not always taken a nonviolent approach in handling my frustrations as a child or as an adult. Let me tell you the truth without giving you a heart attack. The point is, we are not always comfortable telling the truth. We are especially uncomfortable revealing the truth when we fear repercussions.

Where do people feel safe enough to tell the full truth? People are living in houses with people they are not honest with them. I have lived with other people and kept the truth as my secret. I didn't want to be reminded of my truth every day. I wanted a place of refuge and solace from the intensity of whatever was bothering me. Sometimes, I didn't tell because the people in my house were causing me the most discomfort. At other times, I didn't tell because I feared they would not understand me, and would not extend grace to me based on past experiences concerning truths they did not like.

How do I continue telling the truth in a society and atmosphere where the truth-tellers get attacked, and the liars are considered politically correct? When someone

F. Y. I.

asks how I am doing, I sometimes lie and say I am fine when in reality, I am not fine. Do I want to avoid being held accountable for managing my mental and emotional health? I have avoided being checked on. Am I avoiding showing weakness because I have a strong reputation? Am I avoiding showing anger because I have a peaceful reputation? Am I avoiding showing an emotion that contradicts the normal emotions people have expected from me?

If my supervisor asks how I'm enjoying the job, and I am not enjoying it at all, I feel pressured to say that I am. If my spouse asks if I'm enjoying the relationship, and I am not, why do I feel pressured to say that I am? If my child asks if I'm enjoying parenting, and I am not enjoying it, why do I feel pressured to say that I am? If my pastor asks me how I enjoyed the sermon, and I did not, why do I feel pressured to say that I did?

I try not to hurt people's feelings. Instead, I should make a conscious effort to tell the truth The real problem with trying to guard other people's feelings is I have to assume what will or will not hurt them. I have to make a judgment call based on what I think I know about the person and how I think my truthful statement will be received and interpreted by that person. Often, I project onto them my feelings and don't really consider theirs. I am learning to allow others to make their own choice in how they respond to my truth.

As you can see, telling the truth can be challenging. Lies are like leaves covering the body. They are easily blown by the wind. Leaves detached from the plant source will become brittle and dry within hours to days. It is not a sustainable or reliable source of covering. It is easy to accept that leaves are not favorable for clothing. For some people, it is not as easy to accept that lies are not able to

F. Y. I.

withstand the tests of time. Flaws they initially covered and concealed are at risk of being exposed at any moment. Telling the truth should be as natural as undressing for a shower or bath. We understand to cleanse ourselves properly, we must be fully exposed. There is no shame in that moment. Perhaps because it is often a moment if isolation. We truly don't have to carry shame.

My younger sons are Judah (eight) and Zion (four). A couple of years ago they were in a phase of life where being naked was funny. They loved to run from the bathroom into my room or around the upstairs naked. They laugh and giggle when they see cartoons where buttocks are shown. It's just hilarious to them. They were comfortable with me and the occupants of our home seeing them naked. Nowadays, however, Judah is starting to keep the females out.

Nevertheless, Judah, Zion, and Izreal (my 2 years old daughter) are all comfortable walking in the bathroom while any adult in our home is naked. Hence, the need to start locking doors. One day, these same little boys will no longer find it funny for me to see them naked. One day, they will no longer be comfortable seeing me exposed. One day, they will cover their private parts. Sometimes I wish that day would hasten along! My prayer is for them to cover their private physical parts, but still be comfortable exposing their emotional private parts to me. I don't want them to grow ashamed of their private thoughts and feelings, regardless of what they are.

Younger children are not ashamed of their nakedness. I think it's partly because they haven't started comparing themselves to others. How can we return to the days where we are also naked and unshamed?

F. Y. I.

I hate keeping secrets…

    I am a great confidante, and I know things about people I would never repeat. I believe in honoring people's requests and trust in me to be a confidential outlet. I do not mind safeguarding people's vulnerabilities. What I absolutely detest is having a personal problem and feeling pressured to keep it a secret. If I need help, I want to ask for help. If I'm failing, I want to admit to someone that I'm failing. If I'm frustrated and confused, I want to be free to say that instead of feeling as if I have to keep my weaknesses secret. How can I ever get stronger if I do not admit I am weak? How can others help me if they do not know I need help?

    Sometimes, I think people want GOD to show others we need help. We would rather employ GOD to send a divine message or revelation to someone that we need assistance as if GOD is not already busy enough taking care of impossible situations while we are fully capable of communicating with another person. We have the capability, but do we house the capacity? We know how to talk, but do we know how to talk about what feels awkward to say?

    I think about social media and some of the people that come across my newsfeed. I have people that post every emotion they have. If they're hungry, they post it. If they're tired, they post it. If they're angry, they post it. If they're frustrated, depressed, excited, happy, they post it. I watch how people respond to someone angry versus someone depressed. I watch how many more comments and reactions people get when they are bashing someone else, versus revealing something sensitive about themselves.

F. Y. I.

I had a particular friend on social media that I know from grade school. I found myself getting very agitated with his posts in my newsfeed. It seemed as if everything he posted was negative and depressing. Every day, multiple times a day, he was complaining about women being no good. At first, I would comment from time to time and suggest he connect with a different type of woman than those he's previously chosen. He would like the comment, and then the next day, he was back to the same complaints and depressed mood. One time, I sent him a personal message to check on his well-being. He said he was "ok," just working through some "stuff." I offered to support him and be there to encourage him sporadically.

As time went on, he continued in the same rants, and I was just tired of seeing them. It was either post about unfaithful women, disloyal friends, or drugs. I remember thinking; maybe I should unfollow him or delete him. I questioned why I was so annoyed with him expressing his truth. I wasn't sure if it was because I didn't agree with it, couldn't relate to it, or understand it. I figured it out. I was uncomfortable for him because he was not ashamed. I was ashamed for him. I was projecting my shame onto his life and it was wrong. I was accustomed to seeing people's lives through the politically correct filter and not naked and unashamed.

I do not make a habit of following people who are more negative than positive. I do not like the energy involved. It does not bother me that they are honest. I have negative thoughts and experiences myself. I am learning to let people be free. If they show their true nature, then others who love them can work with them towards a new perspective and plan.

Therefore, are you ready to take off the masks, filters, camouflages, and cover-ups, and to become

F. Y. I.

emotionally naked? You may not be ready to start with the world, but you start with the people in your home; or your inner circle. You can be completely honest with your family and friends. I admit it is scary because I may not want their perceptions of me to change. You may have the same hesitations.

I venture to think I'd prefer them to perceive me as I am, and not as they want me to be.

This way, they can witness my true evolution and process, instead of thinking my life is any easier or better than theirs. I am naked and unashamed.

Life happens to us all, but only some of us happen to life.

F. Y. I.

Chapter Two

Perfection Almost Killed Me

"Perfection is not my status: it is my goal."

Perfection became my personal motto almost ten years ago. This goal nearly destroyed me. As a child, I drew many conclusions early on concerning how I did or did not want my life to be when I became an adult. I had examples of people I wanted to emulate and people I wanted to avoid emulating. I devised a plan in my mind of what the perfect path would be and the perfect life. I knew I would achieve and attain that perfection. I became very involved in my faith. I read the Bible from beginning to end, multiple times as a teenager. I changed my language. I changed the music I listened to, and even the television shows I watched. I avoided certain activities that would risk my perfection. I had to be in control of myself at all times.

As a young adult, I immersed myself in church and ministry. I prayed with a group of young people every morning and evening. I was at every Sunday service, Bible study, revival, training, etc. I made up in my heart and mind that if I did everything right, I would avoid certain situations and tragedies in life. I felt that if I only sowed good seeds, I would only reap good experiences. I felt that I could work my way into GOD's favor and grace. In high school, I had a "school mom" Mrs. Linda Pierce, who named me "Little Baby Jesus." This is how serious I was. I wanted to prove that if I tried hard enough, disciplined

F. Y. I.

myself enough, that I too could reach perfection. This may seem humorous to some, but I have changed over the years.

I joined the United States Army in 2002, and I was the perfect soldier. I got perfect scores on my physical fitness tests. I went to the boards and performed well, reflecting greatly on my leaders. I accomplished every mission and task assigned. I was promoted at the earliest times possible. Two years into the Army, I earned three promotions and became a sergeant. I was twenty years old leading people who were older than I was, and some were even making more money because they had been in longer.

I was doing so well that leaders helped me get a four-year scholarship to earn my Bachelor's Degree. I went to college, and I started off with perfect grades. My life was great. I walked onto the cross-country team and earned another scholarship. I made some amazing friends, people I am still connected to over fifteen years later. I also had a map when I would get married and begin a family. I graduated, commissioned as an officer, and became a registered nurse.

A year out of school, I got engaged, bought a house, and got married. I was blessed with my oldest two children, Destiny and Daniel Jr. They moved in when they were five and six years old. A few months later I was pregnant with Judah. We launched our church, and a couple of months later we were leading two churches. My Army career was still doing well. I was a great nurse since my annual evaluations were very high. I was still dotting every I and crossing every t. I was still trying my best to be a perfectionist by being the best Christian, wife, mother, nurse, and soldier. But life began happening, and my perfect life was not so perfect. Oh no! What was I going to do? I'd worked my entire life to get to this place of being a perfect adult, and something wasn't right.

F. Y. I.

Perfection was my goal. Perfection was my goal. What could I do to make the imperfect parts of my life perfect? I could ignore the small problems and focus on the successes. Consequently, I continued to overcompensate at work, church, eventually back at school, in business, and with family. Everything I could control, I did. I achieved close to perfection. I completed graduate school with a perfect grade point average, through a move and two pregnancies. People were calling me a "superwoman." So many asked, "how do you do all of this?" Countless affirmations like "I'm so proud of you girl!" And so many were being inspired by me to also do great things for themselves. I would hear comments like "I want to be like you when I grow up." That comment makes me cringe. No! Don't be like me! Haha! Striving for perfection and maintaining a perfect life can be so unhealthy when your definition is off.

Every time I was faced with an area of imperfection, it devastated me. I would literally die inside. I had to determine a way to fix it. I could not handle my life not being perfect, even when it wasn't my fault. Ugh! I have learned that bad things happen to "good" people just like they happen to "bad" people. Situations arise whether you "deserve" them or not. Good people make bad decisions some times. Smart people make unintelligent decisions some times. Life situations arise to help you grow, not always as a consequence or punishment for being "bad."

For years, I planned how I wanted my future to be, and it was not going according to my plans. I had done everything I knew to do, and it still was not working. After ignoring problems for years, I finally decided to confront them. The ironic part was I didn't need to confront them. I needed to confront ME. Of course, I did not face me. It was

F. Y. I.

easier to face "them." It was easier to be angry with people, and their actions, and what they did to me, and how they treated me. I could avoid any ownership and pain while I was angry. I could avoid any weakness and vulnerability while I was angry. Therefore, I decided to stay angry. I was angry with people. I was angry with GOD. And most of all, I was angry with myself for not being perfect.

I withdrew from crowds and became selfish. I worked on me. I worried about me. I looked out for me. I decided my new purpose would be getting what I wanted. I became distant and unemotional. I was isolated in my own world…and I loved it. I was back in control. I was back at peace. I was back enjoying myself. I was going to work, going to my office, staying in my office, doing my work, and going back home. I detached myself from everything, but my children. I could look at my phone bill for a month and see where I made only a few calls. I would text family once every week or every two weeks. Some friends I would text a couple of times a month, or maybe every few months. I completely enjoyed the holidays with the family, and I enjoyed going back to my own world afterward.

I was quite possibly depressed, but highly functional and honest as much as I could be. The reason I needed the walls of anger and distance was because I imprisoned myself in perfection. My definition of perfection was so off; it literally destroyed my life from the inside out.

I scolded myself so much that I froze. I reached a point where I couldn't make a decision. I didn't trust myself to make any important decisions. I wasn't sure if I would choose the right one. In my mind, one had to be right, and one had to be wrong. I found angst trying to guarantee I know which one was which. I didn't know whether to follow my feelings, which of course could

F. Y. I.

change. I wanted GOD to crack the heavens and tell me. I remember literally asking, "Can I get a burning bush[3] with a voice giving me the answers?" I really wanted to know with absolute certainty.

It was like standing in a burning building and having to choose which exit route I would take. I know I have to get out of here immediately, but do I jump out the window or run down the hall? The longer I remain indecisive, the wilder the fire grows. Is someone going to rescue me? Does anyone even know I'm in here? How could they?

I talk about me because I want you to lower your guard and see that you are not the only one afraid to fail.

Failure is not the worse option, never trying is.

Your life does not have to be perfect. No one's life is. That is the misconception stifling so many of us. We believe that there are actually people who are living perfect lives. No matter how many perfect areas of life someone has, there is always one or two areas that are not. If people were really honest, you would see they are not perfect and their lives are not perfect either. I'm not perfect! My life is not perfect! Believe me.

I listen to wealthy people who give warning, with wealth and popularity comes many concerns that are unpleasant. I listen to couples I think have the perfect relationship and discover before they reached their current place, they went through some serious issues. I listen to business owners who are thriving and find out how many other business ventures they started prior to the one that's

F. Y. I.

successful, and realize they didn't get it perfect the first time either. I listen to parents who have great relationships with their children, and children who are successful, and find out both parents and children made mistakes along the way and would also change some things if they could.

No one has this picture-perfect life we are pursuing. The delusion that someone has a life where EVERYTHING is exactly perfect will rob you of ever being happy and content with your life.

We all have that one area, or more, that keeps challenging us. As annoying, frustrating, and agitating as it may be, it's there to keep us growing.

After years of living behind my wall, I slowly let my counselor into my thoughts. I actually had three women in my life collectively help me to consider removing my walls. They all worked from different angles, and like a combination lock, the collaborative effort unlocked me. The first level of the opening was to admit that **I no longer trusted myself**. Therefore, my ability to trust others was disabled. I did not trust my judgment because I was disappointed that I did not prevent problems in life from happening to me. The second level of the opening was to accept that **I am not supposed to be perfect, not in my works at least**[4]. The righteousness and approval I was longing for, cannot be achieved by works. It is only achieved and maintained by faith, so instead of perfecting myself, I shifted my focus to perfect my faith. This allowed me to extend grace to myself and not condemnation. I had to set a distinction between excellence and perfection. The third level of the opening was to **allow myself and others**

F. Y. I.

to be loved in our imperfect states. If I am able to love an imperfect person, then I will have confidence someone will also love me in my imperfection. The standard is no longer perfection. The standard is honesty.

One example of this is Judah and Zion, early in the morning when they come in my room and I haven't brushed my teeth or washed my face, and my hair is all over my head. They say, "Good morning, Mama. You look so pretty." Or one of the funnier statements, "I like your hair mama." Or one of my favorites, "You're the best mom ever." I still discipline them. I still hurt their feelings, and yet they do not rate me for what I do. They rate me for who I am. They wake up every morning loving me, being affectionate to me, and admiring me.

Redefine your perfection…

I used to think that perfection would be avoiding negative experiences or emotions. Never having an argument or disagreement would be perfect. Never having a financial setback would be perfect. Never having a health concern would be perfect. Never having challenges and opposition would be perfect. I was apparently doing too good of a job making my life look perfect, and it was creating envy in the hearts of others. However, that envy could have been avoided if I was honest with just how imperfect my life was. Perhaps, if more people were open with their imperfections, others wouldn't feel so much pressure to attain a status that hasn't been attained by anyone. I don't feel we share the full story; instead, we share one or two favorable or unfavorable angles as a persuasive argument instead of an informative unbiased

F. Y. I.

presentation. I often say I wish married people would have told me the FULL story before I got married, so I would know what normal was or wasn't. I wish the Army recruiter would have told me the FULL story before I signed that contract and shipped off to basic training. I wish the instructors at school would have told me the FULL story before I graduated and became a nurse. I wish pastors and first ladies would have told me the FULL story before we took over a church. I wish the entrepreneurs would have told me the FULL story before I paid the startup fees.

The reality is, you will never get the FULL story before you begin something. Not even GOD gives out the full story when HE gives you your assignment, purpose, or goal. We know the beginning and the end, but often the details of our journey are discovered along the way. Some say HE leaves it out because HE knows we won't go if we knew the full story. I cannot disagree with that option at all. I know there are some things I would have said "No, thank you" to if I'd known the full story.

I have failed in many areas, almost every area at some point I feel. I have failed exams in the process of obtaining degrees. I have failed a course and had to retake a summer course in undergraduate school. I struggled so much in my junior year that when I asked my former professor for a recommendation letter for graduate school, she was shocked at how well I was doing academically. I barely made it through some courses in my nursing degree. When I graduated from Columbus State University, I wore a yellow shirt that said "Peace!" on it. I was ready to go. I had survived, but I did not excel as I wanted to.

Nevertheless, I learned from that experience that it didn't matter that I failed a course. It didn't matter that I failed exams. It didn't matter that I changed my major and had classes every summer. It didn't matter that I wanted to quit.

F. Y. I.

Regardless of all my setbacks, I earned my degree. And guess what? NO ONE ever asked me my grade point average when I began working as a nurse. No one cared about my grades until I wanted to go to graduate school. Now, I'm in a doctoral degree program, and again I have failed exams. I have failed clinical simulation labs and had to repeat them. At the end of each semester, however, my final grades have been passing. I am learning how to apply my knowledge in clinical practice.

You see, failure doesn't negate the possibility of success. It often sweetens it.

I was using perfection as my term of success. However, I began learning that success and perfection are often not synonymous. I want to succeed in life but my definition of success was all so wrong, and I have suffered mentally because of it. I tore myself down so low that I became vulnerable to the abuse of others.

Today I am comfortable admitting that I have failed in every area of my life. I have failed financially. I was so conditioned with being poor that when I was blessed with a good salary, I spent all of my money. I wasn't investing in my retirement fund. I wasn't investing in anything honestly. I was living for the day. I rarely spend much money on myself, especially not with five growing children. I bought my first home when I was twenty-six, and I was house poor. I paid my mortgage and utilities but went through times when I didn't have anything more between paydays. I have overextended myself with excessive car payments and been in over $300,000 in debt between mortgages, car notes, and student loans. However,

F. Y. I.

I've managed a good credit score, but when I had late payments my credit score suffered for several years afterward. I have lived with no money in my savings accounts even when I was earning thousands. I was failing. Looking good, but failing.

I have failed in friendships. I have lost some special people because of pride, lack of communication, and lack of forgiveness. I have been immature and selfish at times, and I have not understanding of the other person's perspective. I have thought more highly of myself than I should have, and in efforts to protect myself from getting hurt, I pushed people away before they could hurt me. No, I never intentionally tried to hurt anyone, but I can admit, there were times my friends needed me, and I wasn't there. There were moments I could have called or texted to check up on friends or family but didn't. I have people I may never talk to again in my life, not because I stopped loving them, but because I failed at extending grace or reaching out.

Some of you reading this and know me now may be wondering what in the world is she talking about? Yes, I am a great friend now. Yes, I am an encourager, and I try to inspire as many people as I can. Yes, I am kind, gentle, and loving. I am also human, and the general public doesn't have access to all of my emotions or vocabulary.

I have failed in romantic relationships. I took a long time to speak up when things were not going well in marriage. I tried to hide problems until they were beyond repair. I tried to forgive and move on but never could forget the heart-breaking moments. I didn't always communicate with my spouse about how severe my emotions were; instead, I shared it with others. I tried my best to be perfect for as long as I could, but when I realized my efforts were not changing the situation, I gave up. I was still physically

F. Y. I.

present but emotionally checked out. I was guarded and refused to be vulnerable or have intimacy. I was determined not to be hurt again and prayed for GOD to fix my spouse. Eventually, I decided I needed GOD to fix me too. I couldn't see how broken each of us had become. All I could see was what the poor choices were causing me. All I could see were the failures. All I could do was feel the frustration and anger, and even hatred for the experience of failure in my life.

In my mind, everything I did on my own was successful, everything except my relationship with him. In my efforts to shield him, I left him exposed spiritually and emotionally. Of course, he was responsible for his own actions and decisions; however, marriage is a team effort. One person can't win while the other person loses. Either we both win, or we're both losing. At this time, I realized I had failed to maintain my personal health, mentally, emotionally, and spiritually. When I lost myself, I just could not invest anymore.

I never stopped being committed and honoring my vows. I went through better and worse. I went through sickness and health. I went through richer and poorer. And I intended to remain committed till death did us part. Unfortunately, I learned that not every death is physical death. While I could argue about whose fault it was, the reality is we both failed. Before I experienced that dark place myself, I can honestly say I never understood how it could happen.

I have even felt as if I failed as a mother. While my children may not agree, or at least, I hope they wouldn't, there are times I didn't give them my best self. There were times when I was short on patience and didn't communicate in the most loving way. There were times I was too busy and didn't give them the attention they

F. Y. I.

needed or wanted. There were times they were hurting emotionally, and I didn't recognize it. Parenting is a lifelong classroom. I don't know if I'll ever get it just right, but I have redefined success in that area for myself. It's not dressing them in the best of clothes or taking them to the most spectacular places. Success as a mother is instilling in them self-confidence, self-esteem, self-respect, and self-awareness needed to ground them in an ever-changing world. It's teaching them how to pull on the SOURCE, GOD, for everything they need. It's teaching them they are loved no matter what they do, who they become, or where they find themselves. It's producing open-minded people, who have no prejudice, racism, or hate for humanity. Success is filling their minds and hearts with the necessary ingredients to navigate their ways through life, and not fear failure as long as they are trying.

I have failed in business ventures, losing thousands of dollars. I have failed at one point in everything I am succeeding in now. I write this simply to encourage you that you are not alone when you feel like you're failing.

Failure I can handle; quitting I won't tolerate.

Now that I have you doubting whether or not you need to continue reading this book, or if I'm qualified as an author to help you, take a moment to breathe. I could provide a list of celebrities that have failed their way to success, but I think you get the point.

It is not a detriment to your identity to find some areas in life more challenging than others.

F. Y. I.

When I say fail, what I mean is, I have not achieved my intended goal. I can handle failure now, but I won't tolerate quitting. Quitting is the act of giving up before exhausting one's full ability, capacity, or capability. Quitting often happens when we are uncomfortable and reaching our predetermined limits. When I go to the gym to exercise by myself, I push myself to my limits. Ironically, when I go to my Cross-Fit class, my coaches can get more repetitions out of me than I think I have to give. They see me not using my full potential and push me until I completely exhaust myself and reach muscle failure. I don't quit; my muscles fail. That's the goal though.

When working to increase your physical strength, the goal is to reach muscle failure.

One of many things I've learned about functional fitness is my workout is not effective if I do not fully exhaust the muscle groups involved. When you're working for looks, you can get by with lighter weights and more repetitions and never reach muscle failure. On the contrary, when you're working on strength, you have to go for your maximum capacity each time. We literally keep adding weight to the bar until we can't lift it anymore. It's something that I was timid with at first. I didn't want to get hurt, so I was reluctant to add weights. Then, my coach began telling me when to add. I can't say I loved the extra attention initially. I didn't like it because I felt as if she was making me work harder than other students in the class. And she was. She knew that I was stronger than I thought I was. She knew the other students were at their max, but I

F. Y. I.

was not. I couldn't compare my bar to theirs. Some would have heavier weights, and some would have lighter weights, but we were all giving our best effort. Once I started pushing myself for my new personal record at each class, I became stronger. Now I push myself till I feel as if I can't do any more repetitions. And guess what? As soon as the class is over, I magically walk to my car and feel just fine. My body tricks me into thinking it can't do any more until the clock stops, and it's over. That's when I determine how much I've pushed myself. I measure how long it takes me to get out of the gym and into my car.

A small disclaimer for those who do not exercise, muscle failure is not pushing your body until you collapse. We push through discomfort but stop with pain. We prepare our bodies with nutrition and hydration before, during, and after workouts to remain healthy. Isolated muscle groups are targeted to perform as many repetitions as possible. The cardiac muscle is not one we press for failure. Likewise, in your life, there may be isolated areas where you are experiencing failure. Your heart, mind, and spirit should never be on that list.

Now that you have learned about my successes despite the many failures I've experienced, I hope you too will take a moment to redefine your idea of success. Evaluate what concepts are imprisoning you in your life. What words do you use that create anxiety and inferiority in your mind and heart? You have to identify the links forming your chains. This way, you cannot just break them, but destroy them for yourself and for those you influence as well.

Perfection is not my status, and it's not my goal either!

F. Y. I.

Chapter Three

The Blame Game…it's GOD's fault

I have been through varying levels of hardships in my life. I realize that trying to compare scars with others is just a ridiculous catastrophe because we all have different capacities and limitations mentally, emotionally, and spiritually. I understand what one person calls devastation; another person may find it to be a small problem. It is all based on our perception and our varying degrees of difficult moments. Without creating a reason to feel sorry or empathetic for me, I will say there have been some difficult moments in my life where I was utterly broken. I have not been shattered by the doings of any person, but rather the moments where I felt as if GOD let me down.

For those of you who have faith in a Sovereignty, greater than yourself, faith becomes the glue that keeps our lives together when everything before us is falling apart.

Faith is a force that cannot be reckoned with. When it is in full strength, it has the ability to perform the impossible and supernatural events transpire.

Faith is powerful. It fuels belief in our thoughts that overflows into our speech and actions and takes us to great levels. Faith is the confidence we have that nothing is ever

F. Y. I.

impossible. For me, faith had become a refuge and safe haven. When people disappointed me, I went to GOD for strength. When people betrayed me, I went to GOD for comfort. When people hurt me, I went to GOD for healing. When people did anything negative in my life, I ran to GOD. HE is my heavenly FATHER and my SOURCE. Whenever life became difficult, I was always secure because I had a strong foundation in faith. But what do you do when it's GOD that disappoints you?

I know many people say, "Don't question GOD." But I have found myself questioning GOD. I had questions that no one else could answer for me. I was searching for understanding and for peace in the midst of my life's storms. When I prayed and prayed for GOD to fix situations in my life, sometimes they just continued to get worse, and I didn't know what to do. I would fast, pray, and believe, but the situations would not improve. After a while, I decided I was wasting my time praying about it. I felt GOD wasn't listening to me anymore. HE didn't care how I felt. HE wasn't even paying me any attention. Where was HE? Why was I putting all this effort into living "right" if I was going to continue suffering in the process? My faith walk became a contradiction to the way I lived for many years prior to that season.

I became angry with GOD. I stopped talking to HIM. I stopped looking for HIM. I stopped spending time with HIM. I shut down completely. I resolved to become my own reliable source. I was not going to depend on anyone else to meet my needs. I would do everything for myself. HE allowed me to find "success" in my numbed world. I was still excelling in the public eye. HE allowed me to find refuge in the walls I built around my heart, blocking HIM and everyone else out.

F. Y. I.

I can be really stubborn when I want to be. At that time in life, I wanted to be in control. I wanted to feel secure, safe and protected. For that reason I became independent. Looking back in hindsight, I realize what I did was equivalent to one of my children getting angry with me. They are still living in the house I have provided, eating the food I have purchased and prepared, and using the electricity and water for which I'm paying. They may come into the house and stay in "their" room without talking to anyone else, but as independent as they think they are being, they are still relying on me to provide.

What I have discovered while I was having a temper tantrum with GOD is that HE heard every prayer. HE was already orchestrating the change I pleaded for, but HIS timeline was longer than what I desired or expected. Time is the something we cannot purchase or attain more of. We have an appointed time to be born and to die, and it can be frustrating in the middle of those two appointments to get everything accomplished as quickly as we would like. Nevertheless, I am encouraged that GOD, knowing far greater than I do, understands exactly what processes we all need to encounter to produce the final fruit we are all looking to possess.

Whenever I reflect on the moments I felt at my lowest, thinking I was in places I didn't deserve to be in, I am amazed. I do not understand why I had to go through it until I get that phone call, message, or encounter and I find someone in that exact place. When the words, "I know exactly where you are and how you feel because I have experienced that." come out, I smile. In those moments, every negative emotion I had concerning the experiences becomes a lesson and road map to help guide others out of the darkness and into the light.

F. Y. I.

I would love to say that I always received exactly what I prayed for, but I would be lying to you. Sometimes GOD said no. Even some very good prayer requests, such as the healing of people I absolutely loved have not all turned out the way I had hoped for. Nothing is as permanent as death. How does someone recover from that disappointment? My first step is to stop being selfish because I didn't get the miracle I wanted, but I was not the one suffering physically, no matter how much compassion I had. No matter how willing I was to take the pain for my loved one, I could not. Isn't it strange that many times the person suffering from the illness tells us they are tired and ready, yet we persist with what we want? No matter how much extra time we get, it will never be enough. We will never be comfortable letting people die because we know it's permanent. We will not experience them again on this earth, and we can become very selfish.

I do not understand every scenario of death. What I do understand is the grief and heartache. I do understand the brokenness that occurs. I do understand the desire to make it someone's fault. I do understand the desire to release hurt feelings on a targeted canvas. Sometimes, it is someone's fault. Sometimes, it is a scenario where it is preventable, controllable, etc., but for some reason, it still happened. In those moments, we have the right, to be honest with every emotion and thought that comes through our hearts and minds. As we work through all of that, we must find our way to a place of acceptance and peace.

Accepting life doesn't mean you agree with it. Accepting tragedy doesn't mean you agree with it. Choosing peace does not mean you stop hurting or caring or being affected by it.

F. Y. I.

Friend after you stop being selfish, then take a higher view. Often, we magnify our problems to GOD, instead of magnifying GOD to our problems. We make the problems appear bigger than GOD and get angry when HE does not answer at our beck and call.

Whenever I fly, I always request a window seat. I love looking out of the window during the flight and leaning on it when I'm tired. Every time I fly, I am amazed at how much more I can see at once. Most buildings, cars, and surrounding infrastructures appear much smaller. I can see for miles around a city or region at the same time. It puts the world in perspective for me with GOD's view. HE sees the past, present, and future all in the same view. While we stand on the ground looking up at the mountain, HE sits on the throne, looking down on the full picture. HE knows the destination. HE knows the details. HE knows the qualifications necessary not only to reach that place but to occupy it successfully. HE knows which muscles need strengthening, and the exact exercise to stretch and build it up. HE knows the character traits we're lacking and how to buff us with sandpaper until we're smooth to the touch. HE knows how to correct our character flaws. HE knows what's behind that door we're so anxious to enter, and how it will consume us if we are ill-prepared to enter. GOD knows the end from our beginning[5]. At some point, we have to realize that trusting HIM to direct our path is our best option.

As a person who can admit I am a Type A personality, I value being in control. However, when it comes to the ultimate preservation of my life and unlocking my full potential, I have to trust the MASTER to get out of me everything HE's placed inside me. As children, we don't always understand our parents' capabilities or our

F. Y. I.

own. I always laugh at my children when they realize for the first time I can do something they didn't expect. The shocked expressions are priceless. I enjoy their expressions, even more, when they are afraid to try something, and I push them to try despite their hesitation. Afterward, the look they have once they succeed is priceless. It can be as simple as climbing a rock wall and hitting the bell at the top. It can be riding a roller coaster for the first time. It can be making a difficult shot on the basketball court or learning to cook something successfully. Whatever it is, I enjoy witnessing the moment they realize they are stronger, braver, more powerful and amazing than they thought. In those moments, their confidence is built and fortified. It means more than me just telling them. They believe more strongly because they have experienced it. And GOD treats us the same way. HE allows us to experience situations we thought we never could handle and still thrive. HE exceeds our expectations, not by always giving us what we ask for, but giving us what we need and ultimately value more than our original request.

If you could be honest with yourself, there are some prayers you prayed that you can thank GOD for not answering! I have prayed some things in the heat of my emotions that I really appreciate GOD not granting. I have prayed for what I really thought I wanted and needed, only to find out it was not at all what it appeared to be. For example, you look on social media and see your crush from grade school and immediately begin thanking GOD you got away from them because they turned into something you could not even imagine back then.

Seriously though, everyone should stop being selfish. You can change your viewpoint and learn to be grateful. If you ever want to find the favorite in the bunch, look for the one who shows the most gratitude. I don't have

F. Y. I.

a favorite child, yet I don't love them all the same. I love them all just as much, but I love them differently because they are different. My children are overly indulged, code for spoiled. I can admit that. Sometimes, I pray for wisdom on how to provide the life I want for them without removing their understanding that they are truly blessed. My teens understand more than my younger three because they have been through more in their lives. They're also old enough to pay attention to other children at school who dress differently from them or live in impoverished homes. They too have experienced times when they didn't get everything they wanted when they wanted it. There was a period when my children were simply ungrateful. They didn't say "Thank you" for general efforts made to provide for them. They would complain about what was made for dinner. They would complain if they couldn't buy another new item at the store even if they had new toys they still had not used since I bought it. They would pout, whine, and cry when I said we couldn't do something that was not in my budget.

In the beginning, I would become frustrated and annoyed with their attitudes. They are definitely living a much more lavish life than I did as a child. They have no reason to complain. Eventually, I realized why they were ungrateful. They took what they had for granted because their father and I gave them whatever they asked for most times, so they didn't value it. Then, when you add grandparents, they were just used to getting so much. They would get so many gifts that they couldn't even remember everything they got. Christmas is one of those times when I just buy too much. I just love watching children unwrap gifts. It's my greatest joy of that day, watching them filled with the excitement and joy of getting the gifts on their list. Every year, I notice how they pile up their gifts and then choose one or two items to actually play with or wear. And

F. Y. I.

sometimes they don't show excitement for some gifts because they're too busy looking for their most important gift request.

To teach them gratitude I began exposing them to more. I took Judah to give out food to families for Thanksgiving. I showed my children how others were struggling to get enough food to eat and clothes to wear. I also started giving them a set cash amount when we went out. I made them realize how quickly money goes when they want to play games, eat out, and experience entertainment. Nevertheless, some of my children are cheap with their money! They will spend all of mine, but they become stingy when they have to spend it themselves. I also began making them work for items they wanted but didn't need.

Last, I began teaching them how their lack of gratefulness hurt me. When they began complaining right after I granted one request and not another, I stopped them and reminded them of what I just did. I began telling them "thank you" when they did/do chores to help me. If it's something I tell them to do, when they complete it without an attitude I thank them. When they help one another, I thank them. When they take the initiative to help, I thank them. Since I've been thanking them more, they thank me more. I learned this because children reciprocate the energy we give them.

We are GOD's children, but sometimes, we fail to reciprocate the energy HE gives us. It is our responsibility to express our gratitude to our Heavenly FATHER for all HE provides, moment to moment. The breath we breathe is a reason to be grateful. Tell HIM thank you! The ability you have to read, tell HIM thank you. Your vision and/or hearing is a reason for thanking HIM. We focus on what we don't like, and what pains us most, but we forget to be

F. Y. I.

grateful for everything else. Even in the moments when tears are falling from my eyes, I find peace and joy I cannot otherwise experience when I take a moment to tell GOD thanks.

I cannot promise you that saying "Thank you" will make GOD answer our prayers faster or differently, but I can tell you saying "Thank you" changes your mood and perspective. That elevates your spirit and thoughts. You will learn to feel better even when your requests are unchanged because you are changing.

Sometimes the reason we don't get our request is because we're praying for the wrong thing to change. GOD is not interested in changing everything around you, HE's interested in changing you.

When the teacher is administering the test, he or she does not talk to the students. Often teachers refuse to answer any questions. At my current school, the instructors are not even present during an exam. They send someone else to proctor the exam to keep students from asking questions during the exam. When we feel the most disappointed by the lack of HIS voice or HIS presence, it may be test time.

GOD's desires towards you are good and not evil[6]. HE's working to get you to your intended and expected end, by any means necessary. Trust that HE knows what's necessary. Every human in my life has let me down at some point. I have let myself down at multiple points in my life. If I can be completely honest with, I have been disappointed with GOD. It wasn't because HE failed me or let me down. Sometimes I couldn't always see why things

F. Y. I.

had to happen the way they did, yet there is not one experience I've had that I cannot look back on now and see that it was necessary. Each experience helps to mold and shape me into the person I am becoming each day, and for that progress, I am eternally grateful.

We should take a moment to apologize to GOD for our ungratefulness, complaints, doubts, etc. HE's a loving FATHER, who takes pleasure in providing for us. We should think more highly of HIM, and higher of your relationship with HIM.

Now, take a moment to evaluate whether it was actually GOD who let you down or whether it was your decisions without HIM that didn't give you the results you were looking for. Did you make a situation worse that you asked HIM to fix, after ignoring HIS instructions not to do it in the first place?

Disappointments fade when understanding is obtained.

F. Y. I.

Chapter Four

The Thoughtless Prayer Request

I began using a hashtag a few years ago, "MakeMeWiser," for my inspirational posts, or the life lessons I share on social media. I did not realize what I was doing each time I posted that. I was requesting of life, of GOD, of the universe to make me grow wiser. It seems like such a simple statement and a noble request, but it is such a loaded request.

I grew up depending on my faith in GOD to bring me through the darkest hours of my life. I grew up believing that prayer changes things. I grew up under the impression that when I made a request before GOD that HE would perform the task(s) necessary to give me my answer. I do not believe the same way. At times, when I'm reading the Proverbs of Solomon, I am often amazed at just how applicable they continue to be so many years later.

Wisdom does not have an expiration date, but knowledge does.

I had a petition before GOD for several years. The older I have become, I realize age does not change people

F. Y. I.

as much as I thought it did. I thought there was a magic age where people stopped acting like children, and became responsible adults. So, I asked GOD to make me wiser, help me to understand situations that baffle my mind. Help me to understand what torments my mind. I started realizing that GOD stopped answering my prayers for HIM to move quickly. HE wasn't moving, at least not where I could see. HE wasn't transforming and changing people because I prayed for it. HE wasn't fixing my life. And when I realized that HE was not answering my prayers, I stopped praying. I stopped making petitions before GOD to rescue me from my deepest sorrows, or darkest hours. I was angry with GOD because HE appeared to be answering prayers, just not mine.

HE was silent, and so was I. I held resentment in my heart against GOD, not the people in my life causing the turmoil, but with GOD. Because GOD is powerful enough to humble the proud[7] and make footstools out of enemies[8]. However, I was the one low and stepped on. I felt GOD had forgotten me. There were times I devised my own plans to vindicate myself, and HE would block me. I would get even angrier. How can GOD block me from getting revenge but not block others from hurting me? Is HE an unjust GOD? No. HE was working in HIS own timing, pace, and plan for them. It wasn't until I stopped worrying about what HE would do with them, that I actually began learning.

I Am Not Powerless

I was asking GOD to perform miracles when all I really needed to do was trust HIM and remove myself from the situation. I had to come to the realization that I went through what I did because I allowed it to continue

F. Y. I.

although I did not desire for it to continue. I almost lost my mind and life trying to endure like a good soldier. GOD was not even trying to teach me. I was so determined to prove something to myself and others that I chose to stay outside of HIS will for me. I argued and fought over situations changing. I sought counselors and advisors. I exhausted every means of help, only to realize in the end that GOD was waiting for me to become wiser.

I was seeking wisdom on how to fix the problem, but it was not my problem to fix. The product was not manufactured by me. Wisdom was not toiling over shattered pieces. True wisdom was knowing when to let go and let GOD. I was forcing myself to "trust GOD" because it was what I thought GOD expected of me. Yes, there was a phase where I was worried about what people would say, who would be disappointed in me, who would diminish my value, who would lower my pedestal. However, these fears fade when you're walking through hell alone. I made a covenant with GOD, and I do not believe in breaking my promises.

When I defined unconditional love, I thought it was accepting whatever came my way and still being kind, patient, forgiving, and merciful[9]. I thought it was showing compassion for those who did not deserve it. I thought it was being like my Savior to people. I honestly believed that it was my responsibility to draw others to HIM by the extent of suffering I would endure while still giving pure love. I don't know if you will see this as naïve or impressive, but it is my truth. I was willing to love everyone else unconditionally, but I forgot one person in the process- ME.

In multiple scenarios and relationships, I was failing to learn the lesson GOD intended for me to see. It was the most frustrating time in the world for me. How could I pour

F. Y. I.

out unconditional love to people and find myself hurt in the process? How was that GOD's will for me? I had moments where I would tell my best friend Tracie, "I'm done being a good person. I'm going to be a donkey (but I used the King James Version) just like everyone else. Then they'll know not to play with me."

She always brought me back to reality. She allows me to speak all my foolish comments, and then she simply says *"Chish, we cannot stop being who we are because other people are who they are. We are not good, kind, gentle, loving etc. for the sake of reciprocation. We are who we are because it's who GOD made us to be."* She sobers me in my emotionally drunken moments.

The lesson GOD was trying to teach me for many years is that HE didn't ask me to be HIM. I suffer from a condition that is difficult to identify or think is negative until you really REALLY take your guard down and become open to the absolute truth. I have a hero complex. Some may call it a Savior complex. I have a desire to be a superhero for people, but how is that a flaw? Let me show you.

I began evaluating my relationships. I looked at the people I chose. I looked at the people who chose me. The people I was choosing were broken in one or more ways. Some of them entered my life for the purpose of seeking help, but others entered my life to connect for other reasons.

I looked at one particular relationship. I met this person who actually impressed me at our first encounter. I was amazed at the confidence, boldness, tenacity, and passion exuded in this individual's presentation. His gift was quite amazing and packaged in someone young, which was something I wasn't quite used to. We became friends,

F. Y. I.

and I was equally impressive to him. We talked about our mutual passions, ran ideas across one another for input, and cheered each other along in pursuit of our individual goals. Then, one day, I found out about a situation he'd experienced prior to meeting me that I felt was messed up. He was hurt, but of course, no one just says "I'm hurt." Instead, it's phrased as, "They tried to break me, but I'm going to be even stronger after this." Or "They couldn't handle me." Or "They were crazy! Thank GOD I got away from that one." You know, all the comments that are about the infamous "they" and "them" and no comments about how it is impacting my heart, mind, emotions, perspectives, and perceptions.

This was no different. All in the name of not trying to appear like a victim or as if we are looking for pity, we lie about our true troubles. As a healthcare provider in the military, we do a great deal of trauma training. Each time the trainers emphasize not to get focused on the most visible injury we could see. Some of the most life-threatening injuries are beneath the skin's surface. I carry that concept in my day- to- day encounters. I understand how rare it is for people, or even me, to expose the depth of emotional icebergs. I typically test people out with the very tip of it first to see how they handle it. I give people a safe place to share according to their comfort level. My friend began sharing some of the surface facts, common knowledge. However, I could hear the depth of hurt beneath the surface. He didn't believe that there were people who could or would love him unconditionally. Just like that, it became my aim to prove to them that unconditional love existed and they could experience it. This wasn't the first friend I would have this drive for. I have both male and female friends who have activated my desire to go above and beyond for.

F. Y. I.

I was Super-Chish to the rescue! Or Super-Jas, if you know me from down South. I began showering him with love, and he was in awe. We had our first argument, and I handled it differently from what he was used to. I was livid initially, but I forgave and continued to express love. He failed in some situations, and though I was disappointed, I continued to show love or what I thought was love. What I failed to realize was that I had become an enabler who allowed him to continue beneath his potential because I made everything "okay."

I would mention little hints to really should look inward to find the root of their hurt since it was obviously spilling over into their actions and character. However, I was the safety net, the cover, and concealment, the fertilizer but not the pruner. By the time I realized my aim to save them from the theory "There was no true love in this world" was unsuccessful, I was emotionally exhausted and frustrated. I failed to assess the true cause of the theory and what his responsibility was in the formation of this ill-conceived resolve. I was so busy being a savior that I was in GOD's way of actually being GOD.

Many of us are guilty of that in one way or another. Think about the people you keep loaning money to every other month because they have overextended their finances and need a few dollars until their next payday. Certainly, the first time you give the money, you may actually be helping. But after you become the financial scapegoat, you are enabling them to squander their money and yours. I have done that too, but not anymore, so don't get any ideas. How about that friend that comes to vent to you about how everyone else is doing them wrong? If every time he or she comes, you automatically jump on their "side" and support them against the world, it is quite possible you are not helping your friend address the common

F. Y. I.

denominator...THEM. It could be that individual. Everybody can't be wrong in every situation, every single time. Sometimes, your friend or you are the issue. It's not even that someone has to be right or wrong in the scenario, as much as it is important to realize there are multiple rights and wrongs in any disagreement.

I found myself in this situation with another friend I held very dear to my heart. For over a decade we were close, and no matter what other people said about that friend, I was still supportive. Likewise, my friend was supportive no matter who my opponent was. We had a conversation one day where I offended him unintentionally, and honestly unbeknownst to me at the moment. It wasn't until a later conversation came up where I was in need of support that my friend was using a harsh tone with me, and I asked what was going on. We did not resolve the issue and ended up not talking for months, maybe even a year. I unfriended him on Facebook and went on about my business. When he sent me a friend request after that gap, I was reluctant to accept. I finally accepted but didn't say anything directly to him. Eventually he reached out, and we began talking again, and all was well. We became even closer as we were both going through our own life battles, and we shared ideas and strategies with one another as we navigated towards our victories.

Everything was kosher until we had another moment where we disagreed. He was adamant about why he made the decision he made, and I was adamant about why I felt how I felt in response to his decision. The problem arose when he felt I didn't value or honor the foundation of his decision. In reality, I honored it, but it did not negate how his decision affected me. Until both parties were ready to let down the guard of having to be "right" and open ourselves to understand what the other party was

F. Y. I.

trying to communicate, the conversation went NOWHERE. It just became more frustrating for each of us, and eventually hurtful offenses grew. I tried to explain the way I understand situations is to ask pointed questions and to get answers. I am willing to listen, but I also want to be heard. Then, a comment was made implying it always had to revolve around what I wanted but this time it wasn't happening. I actually smile when I typed that because I felt the same EXACT way about how they were acting. The problem with having friends that are so much like you is the moment they mirror your less favorable characteristics. It annoys me tremendously. However, I was calm and replied "Cool. We're both having that problem," and I walked away. The more I tried to fix it or understand it; the more damage was made. I left him with comments of peace and love and let GOD have it. Did it hurt? Absolutely! Did I cry? Many tears. In spite of that I did learn! After a short reprieve we were right back talking again. We refine each other. It doesn't always feel good when tempers flare, but it always settles with growth and illumination.

Wisdom is remembering that a soft answer turns away wrath[10]. Continuing to argue with someone in defense mode is a waste of time and energy. It is difficult to argue with someone who is not angry too. You should try it sometime. When you feel a conversation escalating, and the tempers are rising, consciously turn your volume down and act calmly. No matter what they say, filter those first responses in your mind, and then say the opposite, such as "You're right, and I see your point." Or "I didn't see it that way at all, but thanks for sharing that perspective with me." Or "I'm sorry that's how you viewed what I said or did. That was not my intent." These comments can disarm the angriest people. Even when you disarm them in that instance, wisdom says, wait to try to make your point until

F. Y. I.

either he/she asks, or you both are completely calm and in great moods.

Super Chish had to learn that it's not her job to make everything ok. It's my job to control myself and ensure that I maintain my character, respect, and dignity despite the temptation to ignore all those characteristics for the sake of feeling victorious in the heat of a moment. I know this is vitally important because this very situation was brought to my attention from a few people I hadn't spoken to or seen in several years. They watched me from a distance as I was faced with many incredibly difficult moments of feeling betrayed, disrespected, wrongfully accused, and devalued. I wanted to explode at times. I wanted to go "South Philly" on a few people. South Philadelphia is where I was raised and the social interactions were a little intense at times. I am literally laughing right now because I remember praying that GOD would let me make an example of just one person. Can you imagine that prayer?

"LORD, I know I'm not supposed to be fighting and cursing and acting like a fool, but if you could grant me a quick pass, so I can box this idiot I'd appreciate it. I promise I won't do permanent damage. I just want to knock her out and walk away. And LORD protect me, so I don't get knocked out because that would defeat the purpose of fighting in the first place. Ok, thank you. Amen"

I hope you can take a moment to laugh at me. Some people think I navigate this life without ever having negative thoughts. I have plenty of thoughts that would shock my readers, but the reason you cannot fathom me thinking this way is because I keep these thoughts in my mind. I don't let them enter my mouth or body. I don't speak it. I don't perform it. Not because I am so righteous,

F. Y. I.

but because I know I am an example to more people than I asked for.

Getting back to the main thought, we do not become wiser by simple osmosis. We become wiser through multiple avenues: reading books, listening to sound teaching, praying for clarity, denying ourselves, and experiencing life. Some lessons I tell GOD I'd rather learn from reading or listening to someone else's experiences. I feel as if HE laughs at me during many of my prayers. My mentor, Faye Dadzie, told me that GOD is preparing me for my true greatness with surgical precision. HE is so strategic, not wasting one experience or event. HE is masterful and knows exactly what tools to use to get the results HE intends from and for me.

I began living my life more fully when I opened my mind to the idea that everything is a lesson. I don't like every lesson, but I am more aware of my opportunities to grow through every experience. I don't know much, but I know more today than I did yesterday. That is my goal. Every day, I want to be made wiser. I have to remind myself this means I will be placed in some very uncomfortable situations. I will experience the full gamut of exhilarating emotions to the emotions that feel like hell on earth. The resolve in it for me, and hopefully for you after reading this, is feeling any emotion is a sign of still being alive.

The true masters of life realize we can't accomplish everything in one day. It is okay to leave room for growth tomorrow.

𝓕. 𝓨. 𝓘.

When you don't make the wisest decision in the moment remember the moment you realized that it was not wise and use it in your next opportunity. I stopped getting upset when I was left in difficult circumstances. I learned how to navigate out of a bad situation.

What are you asking for, but upset when you receive it? Perhaps, you're anticipating a bad day before it even begins. Perhaps, you're anticipating an argument with someone before you even begin the conversation. We make requests without understanding that life and death lie within the power of our tongues[11]. If you say, "I'll never pass that test." There's a good chance you will fail the test the first time. If you say, "I'll never fall in love again." There's a good chance you will block yourself from someone sent to love you. If you say, "I'm broke." There's a good chance your bank account will quickly dissipate even after your income increases. If you say, "Those people can't be trusted." There's a good chance you will attract people who are not trustworthy.

You should understand that prayer is not always the formal conversation you have with the MOST HIGH with your eyes closed, head bowed, and in a posture of humility. Prayers are thoughts. Prayers are words. Prayers are desires. Prayers are the requests our hearts and minds make. We have more informal prayers and informal requests than intentional. We expect the worse. Then complain when we get it.

Prayers are your expectations birthed into actions.

I solicit you for one moment. Take an inventory of the phrases, comments, statements, and context themes you

F. Y. I.

use the most. I can almost guarantee your life reflects the most prominent themes you speak. If you're always speaking negatively, you've requested negativity to take root in your life. If you're always speaking in faith, you've requested faith to take root in your life. If you're often speaking in doubt and fear, you've requested the very consequences you doubt and fear to take root in your life.

We don't get the life we want. We get the life we create.

The more I kept saying, that my life would never change, the more things stayed the same because I gave my life permission to stay the same. When you hear, life and death lie in the power of your tongue; it's more than a wise statement made thousands of years ago. I believe everything that was created, was created with a word[12]. Centuries later, we are still creating everything that is with a word. The idea for everything you see began with a thought. It did not become a tangible object until someone said, "I'm going to make it." Think about how many bright ideas you've had that never manifested. Many of them probably never even tried to manifest.

A couple of years ago I decided to create an additional stream of income. I was intrigued by an online marketing program that paid commissions for each person you got to make a purchase. Before I made one commission, I was speaking to a friend who was also interested in creating some passive income. As I was giving her information about the company and compensation plan, she asked me if I really believed in the company. My response to her was, I honestly am not putting my confidence in this company. I really believe in me. If other people can succeed in this business, I don't see why I cannot. I'm betting on me.

F. Y. I.

I went on to make thousands with the company. She joined, and because she didn't believe she never made one commission. I've seen this repeatedly with multiple businesses, scholastic, relational, and personal endeavors. When we do not believe it will work for us, we talk ourselves out of the opportunity to succeed. Perhaps, the reason why you feel your prayers aren't being answered is that you keep sending up opposing prayers that cancel one another out. When you're having a great day, you speak well of your situation or desires. Then, when you have a moment of discomfort, you speak evil of your situation or desire. I admonish you to speak in one direction. A double-minded person cannot expect their prayers to be answered.

You deserve more than you've allowed yourself to experience. Release yourself from mental traps that cause your confessions to waiver. As I grow wiser, I have learned to tame my tongue and increase my faith. GOD is listening closer than you think. HE's granting your request, the good and the less than good.

Only say what you want to see, even if it's not what you currently see.

Now, it's time to fill your toolbox with everything you will need for life, but it makes no sense to carry tools if you don't know how and when to use them. I pray I can help you, as I help myself.

F. Y. I.

Chapter Five

Demonstrators Post: Know Your Role

I enjoy taking long drives. I've been known to drive 12-15 hours for a weekend turnaround trip and not think anything of it. Driving with my children is different, however, I do not enjoy that. I enjoy long drives by myself. I don't stop until I need gas, and I get food, use the bathroom, and do everything I need to do in that one 10-minute stop, and I'm back on the road. I enjoy the time to think. I listen to great music, but I often like to let my mind drift and explore thoughts I just have been too busy to contemplate. I was driving yesterday and having one of my moments where I ask GOD what is the point of going through all of this nonsense? One of the common comments I get when people are trying to encourage me is, "You are so special." I've grown to detest that statement. *(Inserts rolling my eyes right here.)* What does being special have to do with going through the nonsense? Now, I told you about becoming wiser. Experience can breed wisdom, but what is the use of wisdom? Sometimes, I don't want to learn anything else if it has to hurt to learn it. Then GOD whispered something very simple to me that completely lightened my atmosphere.

F. Y. I.
You were selected to be a demonstrator.

In the Army, when we have our physical training (PT) test, there is a set protocol for how these tests are administered. No matter how long you've been in the Army, you have to go through the same exact protocol with each PT test. The leaders administering the test must read the instructions. During the reading of these instructions, there comes a time when the readers say "Demonstrators Post!" This is where other graders come forward to perform each exercise for the soldiers preparing to get tested.

The role of the demonstrator is to provide a visible example of what the verbal instructions mean. In other words, you are a living epistle[13].

There is a demonstrator for the push-ups and sit-ups. He or she gets on the ground into a good starting position. Then shows how far down the graders expect each soldier to go. Then show how far up the graders expect each soldier to go. He/she shows what form is unacceptable and what actions will get you disqualified. There are actually two demonstrators. One is demonstrating the push-ups; the other is demonstrating the grader's role. The grader demonstrator shows how he/she will count each repetition and what they will do if you do not correctly perform a repetition. The intent is to leave each participant without question on what is expected and to show it is actually possible to achieve.

What does that have to do with me? I know I have been called to be a demonstrator. I can confidently say I'm

F. Y. I.

not ashamed of anything I've experienced. I am very transparent, yet I can be too transparent for some people. My mindset is all of us are going through or have gone through something that we are not proud of. The details may be different, but the principles are usually universal. We live in a time where society focuses more on providing a great image, even if the story behind the image isn't so good. I don't mind showing my great moments captured in a beautiful lens with perfect lighting and a glam squad that make me look flawless. People really like those images, and they draw much attention. I'm also comfortable sharing images of me post-workout when I'm looking "a hot mess." I want to show people the process of achieving those beautiful shots. I told GOD that whatever doors or platforms HE afforded me, I would be willing to share what HE's done for me with transparency. Every time, I grab a microphone or sit in a session to counsel or mentor, I always expose me.

I am a demonstrator. I have been selected to come up front and let people watch me as I go through the tests of life. My foundation of faith is in the Bible. I have memorized many scriptures over the course of my life. I have read it from cover to cover multiple times. Even with that, I know that not everything I've read makes practical sense to me. Whatever your faith foundation may be, or moral compass, I think we've all had moments where we read something that we just couldn't see anyone doing in real life. For example, if someone slaps you in the face, give that person your other cheek[14]. I can remember the very first time I read this passage. My eyes widened and my mind tried to imagine someone slapping me in my face because I normally would not tolerate this. I have fought people regardless of gender and size for putting their hands in my face. Every time I tried to imagine actually living that scripture, I could never get past the first slap. I literally

F. Y. I.

could not make my mind go past imagining someone slapping me without the reflex of slapping back. I was a teenager at the time, and as a woman in my mid-thirties, I still cringe at this scripture. I can at least imagine it all the way through. Now, I cannot say I have literally lived this with a physical slap in the face, but I have lived this principle with the figurative statement, "that was a slap in the face."

I can remember one situation vividly. A young lady was going around saying negative things behind my back. She never said anything directly to my face. Whenever we were in the same room, her body language showed the chip on her shoulder, but she was never bold enough to be direct with me. The problem she had with me is that I was in the position she wanted. In addition, there was another young lady who was friends with the first girl. At first, the friend was a neutral party. She had no loyalty to me. She didn't know me at all, so I wouldn't expect her to. Eventually, the friend took the time to talk to me. I was able to help her through some personal problems, and she realized the type of person I really was. The friend began feeling bad for me. She knew of all the rumors and comments being said that I wasn't privy to. One day, she really wanted to talk to me to let me know what was going on. I remember having to speak in service, and she sat on the front row. I could see how heavy her heart was. As I delivered my message, I took a moment to look her in the eyes and said, "I have learned not to respond to everything I know. I am responsible for my own actions. I trust GOD to vindicate me. HE will repay." She looked back at me with tears falling down her face, and I encouraged her that I was truly at peace.

People are watching you, whether you know it or not. We can respond like "most people" and use the human

F. Y. I.

card to justify our inappropriate actions. Honestly, sometimes, people would rather we come down off the wall[15] and deal with the people taunting us below. It is enticing at times, but the lasting effects tarnish the story. Think about the public figures you respect. Many have been verbally attacked, placed in bizarre news stories, tabloid magazines, rumor mills, and all kinds of media. If they chose to respond to every insult, criticism, or disrespectful comment, they would have no time to actually fulfill their role. They are demonstrators and often represent a cause greater than themselves. Their ability to stay calm under duress demonstrates their character.

I am a demonstrator who gets to show people how to correctly perform an exercise and how to incorrectly perform an exercise. I get to show people how to pass the test and how to fail the test. I am a demonstrator who inspires people that it can be done. I get to discourage people that it cannot be done. I get to show people the easy way and the hard way. I am a demonstrator. It's up to me to determine the quality of demonstrator I am. It's up to me to determine what written WORD I will bring to life. I am not a Savior, and I'm so happy that the burden is off my shoulders. I am not a superhero. I am simply a demonstrator.

Qualifications:

In order to qualify as a demonstrator, you must be capable of the following:

1. Know how to correctly perform the task
2. Be capable of passing the test yourself
3. Be willing to perform with people watching

F. Y. I.

If you haven't learned this about me yet, you will come to understand I am that *"why"* person that annoys everyone. I couldn't just leave GOD alone when HE told me I was a demonstrator. I had to ask why. I wanted to know how I was chosen for this task. I know the right way to live and respond to many situations because I read the manual. I have passed many tests of my character and strength on the backside of mountains and in valleys where no one was there to watch me. I like to think about David when he was preparing to fight Goliath. While everyone was trying to determine what qualified him to fight, he said I fought lions and bears protecting my sheep when no one else was around[16]. He was basically saying, "I've been winning insurmountable fights before you even noticed me. Today isn't my first big fight. It's just my first big audience."

Today isn't my first big fight. It's just my first big audience.

David was a demonstrator. He demonstrated how to defeat giants. He demonstrated how to win wars. He demonstrated how to worship GOD. He demonstrated many incredible accomplishments, especially about keeping a pure heart. Now, what also came along with him demonstrating all of his great victories was the other side of life. He was also caught, demonstrating many of his failures. That's the difficulty of being a demonstrator. We don't get to choose when GOD has us before the audience. David demonstrated succumbing to the lusts of the flesh. He also

F. Y. I.

demonstrated how to be chastised, forgive, and restored.

The beauty of a true demonstrator is that we are maintaining our lifestyles because we are honored to be selected. We are not doing it for the crowds. We are doing it because we want to live a victorious life that is pleasing to the CREATOR. I only use the audience for motivation when I am tempted to step outside of my character. That's when your eyes inspire me to be silent, turn my phone off, to delete the post I've drafted, and go sit down. However, I'm not training to impress an audience. I want to stay qualified to be a demonstrator for positivity. I want to be a light, and refreshing aura in a space where many examples of how to retaliate, "clap back," "snap" and be "ratchet" are rising.

I have two beautiful daughters I am raising to one day be phenomenal women. I have three amazing sons I am raising to one day be extraordinary men. I have a crowd of five in every season of my life. They keep me alert at all times. My youngest two are too young to read this book, but they can understand watching me demonstrate kindness, generosity, patience, perseverance, gentleness, love, etc. They can also understand when I am demonstrating rage, frustration, anger, rudeness, abrasiveness, and other negative attributes.

Whether you can identify your audience or not, just know you are also a demonstrator.

F. Y. I.

Some days, you will be the demonstrator showing the exercises. Some days, you will be the demonstrator showing how the grading is performed. Some days, you may be in charge of reading the instructions. Other days, you will be back in the audience preparing for your own test. In whatever state you find yourself, know your role.

Some people are present to plant a seed[17]. The seed can be a word of inspiration or encouragement. The seed can be a word of negative connotation. The seed can be an act of kindness and generosity that propels a person into their destiny. The seed can be an act of cruelty that creates mental chains around a person's self-esteem and image. Examine your seeds. We all have them. Plant the good seeds in people. Place the bad seeds in a waste can without dirt. I said WITHOUT dirt. We don't want to give those bad seeds an opportunity to grow or draw any nutrients from the soil. That means stop carrying gossip from one person to the next, and ruining people's names as you spread the bad seed sown in your heart.

Some people are present to water the seed[17]. These people are refreshing wells in our lives. They are forever uplifting, pouring out strength, confidence, and wisdom. They admonish you along the journey, reminding you of what your seed can grow into with consistency and perseverance. Water flows. It is vital to every living organism. Identify those who nurture you and keep them close.

If you are present to water, ensure you maintain the purity of the water. Contaminated water creates illnesses around the world every day. Some waterborne illnesses lead to death. Guard your water source. Make sure you don't let anyone defecate in the water. Make

F. Y. I.

sure you don't let anyone throw trash in the water. Make sure you don't let the water get stagnant; it must continue flowing. Connect to the SOURCE, the Living Water.

GOD gives the increase[17] to every farmer. The farmer can plant a seed and work the land. They can water the seed. But the farmer cannot make the seed transform into its true form. That's the role of the CREATOR. While you're living this life, always take a moment to identify your role in a situation. Know it. Learn it. Live it. Then, let GOD fulfill HIS role. This is a guaranteed way to reduce your frustration along life's journey.

It Will Make Sense

There was a man in the Bible who was living in a cemetery[18]. He cut himself with stones. He was insane according to a modern description. He was literally out of his mind and was so disturbed that he could not even be contained or bound with chains. People walked by him, but no one walked near him. He was overwhelmed with so many problems. The story reports he was possessed with a legion of evil spirits. That is not the part of the story that stood out to me. The important part is that the man meets JESUS, and is delivered from all his torment. The man is restored to his right mind. The people from his community are astonished when they see the man sitting normally, fully clothed, and coherent. Who knows how long the man was tormented by this point in his life? It was long enough for his community to resolve his condition as his norm. They assumed he would always be that way, and they were content keeping their distance.

F. Y. I.

What is strange about this story is that the man tried to leave and follow JESUS, but JESUS said no. Why would JESUS tell the man he couldn't leave to be a disciple? In scripture, people were chastised when they didn't leave everything behind to follow GOD. The man was so grateful for his newfound liberty and life that he wanted to serve the man who freed him. Instead, he was told, "no." He couldn't go with the other disciples. He had to stay in his home town. He was instructed to tell the people of his country about what he experienced when he met JESUS.

The preacher in me wants to expound even more on this text. I was somewhat angry when I read this story. It felt las if JESUS was leaving him in a place that was never there to help him. JESUS was leaving him in a place where he had no friends. JESUS was leaving him in a place where people had talked about him when he was tormented. JESUS was leaving him in a place where people laughed at him and ostracized him. JESUS was leaving him in a place where he had suffered publicly. JESUS was leaving him in a place of abandonment and despair. JESUS was leaving him in a dead place since he lived in a cemetery.

I just felt that this wasn't fair. It became personal to me because I was this man. You might be this man too. Have you ever felt as if you were in a place where you were publicly humiliated, embarrassed, hurt, tormented, or troubled? Have you ever gone through a crisis so bad that when you finally came through the situation you didn't want anything to do with the people or place you were in? It's like a business owner having to close his or her shop, but still, go to work in the shopping center where the business failed. It's like a leader who has a moral failure, trying to live in an area that won't let him or her forget what happened. Maybe you've encountered this with your family or friends at some point. You know that you made

F. Y. I.

mistakes and went through the process of correcting them but you had to live in the confinement of what people thought and said about you.

The easiest choice to make is to leave and start over somewhere else. People relocate all of the time. If one city doesn't work out, they move onto the next city and try again. However, what happens when you can't move away from the place you connect with your personal hell? It was as if JESUS told the man, "No, you can't leave with ME. You have to stay and tell these people about the mercy you've obtained. You have to show these people that you are really a new creature. You have to stay to show these people that this wasn't a gimmick or trick. You have to stay and show these people that your life has been transformed, renewed, and set free. Therefore, you can't leave. If you leave, they will forget about you. They will forget about your struggle. They will forget about your deliverance. They will forget the essential pieces that will produce hope when they face their darkest valley. Everyone in that community knew about the man's struggles. He was not a stranger there. He was from there. He suffered there, and he was liberated there.

Friend, you are more like this man than you first thought. You are forced to stay in the place you're eager to escape for good reason. You are a demonstrator! You have to stay connected to all those people you wanted to cut off as a reminder that GOD is still faithful no matter how hard life gets. GOD needs you in your family, on your job, in your community because you are a constant testament for others to see.

Stop trying to run from your hard places. I can admit I've been like this man. I have been ready to run on to a new place after going through hardships in certain cities. There was a time I said I would never go back to

F. Y. I.

particular places because I associated it with negativity. Nevertheless today, I can look forward not only to going back to those places but to connecting with people who knew me while I was going through my hardships. I am honored to show them that it doesn't matter what you go through because you too can make it. Not only can you succeed, but you can flourish after your difficult experience. You are still worth GOD's time, love, grace, mercy, forgiveness, and favor.

No one deserves grace, but everyone needs it.

This message makes all the chaos, suffering, embarrassment, heartache, and drama worth it for me. People are not only watching you suffer. They may be standing by talking. They may even standby laughing and taunting. They may do this because they are not equipped to help you. In fact, they're scared to get too close because they don't want to join you in that hard place. You look like bad luck to these superstitious observers. Just remember, the audience doesn't stop watching when you get to overcome your problems. They continue watching to see if you continue to live successfully. They want to see if you really stay free. Some may look in doubt and disbelief at your change. Some may look in amazement. None will be able to deny the fact you are a new creature.

The man from the cemetery was not permitted to leave because it was time to fulfill purpose. He went through all his hardships alone on stage. What gave him a bad name would be the foundation of his ministry. They will always say, "That's the man that was possessed by the legion." The keyword in their statement is "WAS."

F. Y. I.
I don't care what people say about my past, as long as they put the "WAS" in it!

Friend, stop getting angry when people bring up your past. They are using it as a point of reference for how far you've come. I've learned to laugh when people start with "Girl, I remember when you were…" I can say, "Yes, I remember that! I remember a lot more than you were able to see. We both can thank GOD that I'm far from that person today."

Remove that source of offense from your life. Just ensure they use the "WAS" in everything they bring up. They are listing your old character, identity, and habits because it's obvious you are no longer that person. They may not be able to phrase it correctly, but they are truly amazed at how far you have come. Some may doubt and walk-in disbelief concerning the permanent status of your transformation. That is perfectly acceptable. They weren't living in the torments you went through, and they aren't living in your liberty now that you're out.

Shift your mindset concerning the lot you have been given in this life. You are taking the test that you are qualified to pass. GOD knows your major, even when you don't. When I started college, the registrar asked what my major was. I had to select where I would concentrate, so my advisor could help me select my classes. I chose biology when I got there, but I graduated with a nursing degree. What's my point? I didn't know what I needed to study because I thought I was going into a different job after school. My major changed because I started realizing my biology classes were not aligning with my passion.

F. Y. I.

You may not know your true purpose yet. You may not even know your true identity yet. GOD knows exactly what life lessons you must encounter in order to become who HE created you to be. Today, be a demonstrator!

F. Y. I.

Chapter Six

Use Your Voice: Silent Screamers

Silence pretended to be my strength, but it was my heaviest burden.

At the age of sixteen, I wrote a play entitled *"Silent Scream."* It was not a horror play even with the title. It was inspired by a Darryl Coley song "Silent Scream," that spoke about how many people were suffering from daily, but no one knew because the people were silently screaming. They were muting the sound of their pain. I never actually had the chance to see my play in production because I lost part of the script after changing computers. I still have a few scenes printed out in a binder. One day, I will either make it a book or produce it.

Nevertheless, as I prayed for sensitivity producing this content, I couldn't help but think about all of the "strong" people who are helping everyone else, but no one seems to be helping them. I think about all the coaches that are inspiring every member of their team to do their best, exceed their mental and physical limitations, and be proud of whether they win or lose. I think about all the life coaches helping people who are suffering emotionally and then nurturing them along the path to their new launching pad of greatness. I think

F. Y. I.

about all the parents working hard to provide the best they possibly can for their children, affording them a life the parents never had themselves. I think about all the caregivers for the disabled, ill, or elderly loved ones who cannot take care of themselves. I think about leaders on the job, helping to cultivate an atmosphere of comradery and cohesiveness while ensuring the mission is achieved daily. I think about the school teachers, pouring more time and energy into some children than their own families do while the teachers are living off a less than deserving paycheck. I think about those who serve others, whether in glorious positions or unseen without any accolades or rewards. I think about the counselors, medical providers, ministry leaders, community leaders, activists, members of the judicial system, and those sitting in any position of influence. I think about people in the entertainment industry with the magnifying glass on their every move. I think about all of these people, even those special people raising their grandchildren, great-grandchildren, and other children in order to keep little babies safe. I think about foster care parents and those who adopt. I always think of those who care for others.

I wonder how many of these people are allowed to admit they need help? I'm not referring to perfectionist but those who may be suffering in silence because they have so many people depending on them. The ones that feel guilty taking care of themselves may silence their pain and continue to serve others.

We all know that person who is known as the "rock," whether it's an official title we have given or an unspoken understanding by everyone. In families, you see it very frequently. Sometimes, it's the oldest child after the parents are deceased or disabled. Sometimes,

F. Y. I.

it's the most financially stable person in the group. Sometimes, it's the most outspoken person. Often, it's the quiet one who doesn't say too much, but when they finally speak, everyone knows it is serious and adheres. There may be varying levels of responsibility shared among a small group of family members, but it's a common concept across family dynamics.

We all can identify that person at work that keeps everyone calm when situations get out of control, and everyone is angry. It's the person that brings everyone back together and brings a sense of calm and peace to the chaos by not only their spoken words but also by their demeanor and actions. Maybe, you have that mentor or friend you can identify, who is available whenever life becomes difficult. These may be people you think never have a bad day. Maybe a more accurate account is the person who makes everyone scared if they're having a bad day because it rarely happens. Surely by now, you have either identified yourself or someone close to you in one of these positions. Why does it matter? What does it mean? Well, these are the people at an increased risk of being a *"functional sufferer."*

Functional Sufferer

A functional sufferer is a person, likely suffering from depression and/or anxiety, but the individual does not fit the stereotypical description because they remain productive outwardly. They may be similar to a functional alcoholic who drinks copious amounts of alcohol throughout the day, but their speech isn't slurred. Their gait is steady. They are high performers on the job, and they are clean and well dressed. They don't fit the description of the

F. Y. I.

drunk who smells the alcohol pouring out of his/her skin, who can't hold a conversation with you, and has missed paying bills and eating because he or she has used all their money on alcohol.

I was working in the clinic recently when a male in his early sixties came for a medication refill and general physical. The doctor training me was not familiar with the patient, so we began looking at his medical record to gather any pertinent medical history that would help guide our assessment. We noticed the man had a recent visit to the emergency room for chest pain. This is a serious medical concern, so we looked at the documentation to see if the man had a heart attack or any serious chronic repercussions from it. What we found shocked us. The man went to the emergency room for chest pains, but his bloodwork revealed he was abusing cocaine. We looked further into the chart and saw this was an ongoing problem over at least seven years in his medical record. We looked at his bloodwork for the current appointment and noticed there was damage to his kidneys. Initially, we attributed that to his high blood pressure. Later, we discovered he had multiple risk factors that increased his probability of damaging his kidneys, and cocaine was one.

The medical tech gave us a generic report on the patient. The tech didn't ask about drug use, and the patient didn't offer his history of addiction. When I walked into the room, I wasn't quite sure what I expected to see in his physical presentation. I assumed he would look like the people I have seen on television: emaciated, disheveled, and anxious. Instead, I saw a sixty-year-old man who looked as if he was fifty. He had a fit physique, muscular build, great teeth, smooth skin, well-nourished, and a handsome face. During the interview, I could see why the tech never even thought to ask this man about drug use.

F. Y. I.

Fortunately, I've been taught to ask everybody. It eliminates having to stereotype a patient and affords me the opportunity not to miss a functional alcoholic, drug abuser, or high-risk sexual patient.

The man was married for forty years, had several children, over thirty grandchildren, and even some great-grandchildren. He was working a good job and retired from the military. On the surface, it did not appear this man fit the description of a cocaine addict, yet he was suffering internally with a pain he could only silence with cocaine. My heart dropped because I wondered if his wife ever noticed he was suffering. I wondered if any of his adult children ever took the time to ask their father if he was okay. I wondered how many days he hid away to get high, just to numb himself enough to present a happy, strong demeanor to his family and friends.

I completely understand many of you will say to yourself, "Well I'm not addicted to cocaine." That may be true but are you addicted to something else? Silent screamers find a way to mask, numb, and relieve their pain through some other outlet, whether legal or illegal. I pay attention to the men and women who need to have sex with multiple people at one time and are never satisfied with any of it. I wonder what pain they are trying to cover. Was it a sexual violation? Was it abandonment? Was it trying to prove their sexuality to themselves or others? Was it feeling insecure? Was it seeking validation? Was it seeking love and affection? Where are they really hurting? Sure, sex can be exhilarating for any of us. I venture to say most people who have had a good sexual experience look forward to having more good experiences. However, when you're having so much sex and not protecting yourself or others, the risk of contracting a lifelong sexually transmitted disease is exponentially increased. Now, we're

F. Y. I.

talking about life and death. What is the root of it? Where does the pain start? Who was there to listen, or who was there to silence it? What keeps them bound in silence when their heart is screaming in torment?

Some of us are addicted to material possessions. The spending never ends, even when the money is not there to support or sustain it. The credit cards always have a balance, and the savings accounts rarely do. The latest phones and technological gadgets are upgrading at every turn. The latest apparel has to be paraded across various venues for everyone to see. It's never enough just to get these items. There has to be a public display of them with the glory of admiration and responses from the crowd. Having the most beautiful home in the family may not be enough. Having the most luxurious car in the neighborhood may not be enough. The "dream life" with everything you can imagine may not be enough. What pain is being covered up with materialism? Was it poverty as a child? Was it being teased because you didn't have the top brands growing up? Was it an attempt to prove someone wrong who said damaging words to your heart? Is it a need to feel important? Is money being equated to self-worth?

Some of us are addicted to our careers. We are hard-charging along, getting every promotion at the earliest eligibility. We are getting employee awards of excellence. We are giving 1000% to the job, sacrificing whatever needs to be sacrificed to achieve our next goal. We are not concerned with the casualties, such as our spouses or children, who are being neglected. We are fixated on the prize. The prize, of course, changes every time we achieve one goal. It's never enough to satisfy our hearts. We think, man when I get this position I'll be set. You get that position, and it's great for a few months, but then you're itching to do more. It is hard to distinguish between

F. Y. I.

ambition and emptiness. You're so determined to gain the whole world, climb to the highest level of the ladder, and break that ceiling but it's never enough. What pain is being silenced? Is it fear of being a failure like someone you loved? Is it fear of being like one of your parents? Is it fear of being unstable? Were you forced to move as a child because of financial strain? Did you have to live with other family members because you couldn't afford to live in your own home? Did you grow up in subsidized housing? Were you on welfare? Were you angry because you didn't have the lifestyle or experiences you wanted? Were you hurt because you didn't understand why you didn't deserve what others had? Are you working so hard to be a success at work because you're failing or struggling at home? Are you waiting for compliments, accolades, affirmations, and acknowledgment? What is really driving you?

Some of us are addicted to food. Not every food addict is overweight. Some exercise just as much as they eat to keep it balanced. However, what is the pain that's trying to be silenced here? Are you bored? Are you depressed? Are you creating a wall to isolate yourself behind? Do you love yourself? Have your dreams been shattered?

I was watching a television show about people who were morbidly obese. I'm talking 400, 500, 600, 700 pounds. Each had a different story, but all the reasons they began gaining weight had to do with stress, heartache, or giving up after failing to achieve their major dream. Many of them said they ate as a distraction from their pain. Some ate themselves into their own isolated world where they could not even leave the house.

I could go through a list of addictions from the obvious ones to the not so obvious ones, such as cleaning obsessively. We all have a means that we use to

F. Y. I.

decompress and rejuvenate ourselves. No matter what we choose, moderation and balance are the keys separating healthy and unhealthy uses of that means.

> ***Whether the addiction is ingested, injected, or interactive, it's not an addiction to the vice. The addiction is to the moment of emotional freedom perceived under the influence of the vice.***

More importantly, acknowledging that we are hurting is only one piece of the puzzle. Most people can admit to themselves they are hurting. Sometimes, we phrase it as being disguised angry, frustrated, disappointed, or "I'm good." We certainly have to get comfortable telling ourselves, "I'm hurt."

> ***Can you let yourself be free to feel what you feel without self-condemnation?***

One point I have learned in my life is that I am my worst critic. No one else can be so demanding as I am of myself. For years, I could not even accept a compliment without undermining myself. Whether I did it out loud to the person offering the compliment or to myself when I had time to let my thoughts run free, it was coming. I imagine that you are rather hard on yourself as well, I try to share my mistakes so that I never write in a tone that criticizes you, but I always invite you to be honest with me. It's a judgment-free zone where I show you how I got through the process.

F. Y. I.
Screaming My Heart Out with a Smile

Friend, I can't tell you when exactly my silent suffering started because I honestly got so used to it, it felt normal. I was going along in life doing multiple tasks at once, as is my custom. I never seem to thrive with one goal. The overachiever in me fighting to prove I'm smarter than the prejudice teacher in sixth grade thought I was. I was too busy trying to disprove stereotypes that every Black woman thinks her best assets are her breasts and buttocks, and her ability to satisfy her suitor in bed. I have been prejudged as if our brains aren't extraordinary and our intellect beyond reproach. So yes, I'm addicted to winning, whatever that is as seasons change in my life.

Somewhere between being a wife, mother, graduate student, full-time worker, church leader, mentor, online business entrepreneur, public speaker, author, and inspirational video and flyer poster I started falling. I was literally doing something seven days a week. I was juggling everything well. I was there for my friends when they needed me. I was hosting live events with good crowds. The vision was flourishing. I was sitting with the VIPs and among the admired. My house and cars were impressive. My children were beautiful and I was attractive too, but I was falling.

Eventually, I have had a moment where I was just overcome with tears. It would feel as if it was out of nowhere, just random crying. If I was in church, I could disguise it as feeling moved by the songs or message. If at home, I could take a long shower. If I cried at work, I would quickly get to a bathroom and gathered my bearings. I would have a day of release, and then I would be right back to coasting along. The random crying episodes started every six months; then it was every three months. I began having relapses every other month, then monthly, then

F. Y. I.

multiple times a month. Eventually, it became a daily struggle. All the while, I was still smiling.

I found myself falling deeper, and because I couldn't really pinpoint what was wrong with me, I didn't know with whom to share my troubles. I would talk to my small circle of trusted confidants on specific areas of stress, but no one confidant ever knew everything I was dealing with at once. If they ever got together, they would see just how much turmoil I was really enduring. However, on the outside, I was still doing everything I had been and excelling in it all. I would graduate from my program with a perfect grade point average, publish another book, and be awarded a full scholarship for my doctorate degree.

Nevertheless, life was wearing me down slowly from various sources, but I was still smiling. I started taking fewer pictures of myself because I didn't want my face to show my light was getting dim. When people see you on social media, it's easy to show them what you want them to see and conceal what you don't. I began posting only photos of my children and my inspirational quotes with my professional photos. The people I interacted with on a daily basis, still saw my smile. I would laugh and joke and seem to have a good time. By the end of the day, I would be completely exhausted. I couldn't wait to get home, go to my room, climb in the bed, and not have to smile. I was not only falling, but I was also sinking.

I held myself hostage in my own head from letting people see I was weak. This superwoman had found her kryptonite. I would go on to become clinically depressed. I didn't want to admit that for months. I knew the signs and symptoms, but I did not want that condition coupled with my name. I was Simply LaChish. I could not be depressed. I'm out coaching and inspiring, yet sinking in my own complex situations.

F. Y. I.

I wished I could just deal with a situation and move past it, but it got to a point where it was one crisis after another. It reminds me of when I was in labor. There were times I would have small contractions before the baby was due from dehydration or overdoing my activity for the day. It could just be my body preparing itself for labor. When true labor starts, the contractions become rhythmic and get progressively stronger and closer together. I can remember with Zion the contractions were so close they overlapped. There was no break from the pain; it was every minute until he was born.

Life hit me like that, but when I was pregnant, I knew my pain was purposeful. The pain was just a bi-product of meeting my baby. For that reason, I could endure that pain because I could see a clear ending to it. In life that's not always the case. We cannot always see how our pain is purposeful, nor can we see the definite ending of that pain. We must endure **until** the time is right.

"Until" is the most discouraging place to be when you are in pain.

I found myself with all the symptoms on the checklist for depression. I had difficulty concentrating, sleeping, eating, and maintaining interests. I began to withdraw from everyone. I suffered chronic fatigue and feelings of hopelessness. I cried easily without provocation. I knew I had to seek help when I didn't even want to spend time with my children. I literally had to make myself watch the clock and spend at least 20-60 minutes with them. That's when I knew I needed to admit something was wrong.

F. Y. I.

I'm sure I will make some of my friends and family upset reading this because they would gladly have supported me if I had only said something. I just didn't know how to start the conversation. I didn't want to disappoint them. I didn't want to be judged. I didn't want to be lectured. I just wanted to stop sinking in despair. Finally, I reached out to a mentor and a friend who are both in the mental health arena and followed their instructions to improve my mood and mind.

My suffering was not an indication that I lost faith in GOD. It was not a damper to love and commitment to my family. It was not a reflection of inadequate resources. I simply lost my voice when it came to advocating for myself. I spent years pouring out without a refill, and it finally caught up to me. I was running on empty but felt too guilty to stop at a gas station because I was so busy doing everything all the time. You read at the beginning of the book where it leads me. I'm proud to say today, I am no longer sinking, but I'm swimming. The storms of life have not ceased, but I am fueled for the journey.

Use Your Voice

I couldn't reverse my direction until I shared my emotional condition. My first job in the military was Combat Medic. Of course, the recruiter told me I was a Healthcare Specialist, but the drill sergeant corrected that misconception when I got to basic training. Either way, during my EMT training, I learned various treatments, in particular for trauma patients. As the Iraqi and Afghanistan wars grew more intense and casualties became greater, we moved to teach every soldier how to perform buddy care. Eventually, every soldier was both an infantry person and a

F. Y. I.

medic. Regardless of what our official job title was, we had to learn basic soldier skills and basic medical skills.

You may have seen war movies where a person gets injured, and they yell out "MEDIC!" or "DOC!" The purpose is to notify the person trained to help save lives that you need help. The other benefit of yelling out is helping the medic find the wounded on the battlefield. You have to understand a war zone is not quiet. There are guns firing, grenades launching, and bombs exploding. If the injured person or their buddy doesn't yell out for help, their life could be lost.

I was in an advanced trauma life support course, and the instructors said it only takes 3-5 minutes to die from a major bleed. Considering how important every minute is, the wounded must be proactive in saving their own lives. They must apply their personal tourniquet to their injured limb if possible to stop the bleeding or put pressure on the site. While working to save their own lives they have to yell out for help.

Now consider how loud life can be on a daily basis. People may be all around you, but that doesn't mean they are actually observing you. If you're like me, still wearing a smile on your face, still producing, still moving forward, many will not even notice you are having any trouble. We live in a time where people walk around with headphones to avoid interacting with others, so we are often preoccupied as we pass one another. We may ask how the other is doing, but generally in passing and not really waiting for a true response. The people around you may be dealing with their own problems because you may not be the only injured person on the battlefield of life. However, those who have minimal wounds can help those severely wounded.

F. Y. I.

I completely understand the mindset of a "strong" person. It's a title once worn with honor. It's also a title that caused feelings of reluctance when I needed help. It takes strength to ask for help. Don't be the person we lose unexpectedly because you suffer in silence until you are completely helpless. Tell someone that you need help. You may not get it from the person/people you expect, but helpers are positioned all around you if you speak up and look around. Don't restrict the candidates prepared to help you. It is better to give than to receive, sure. When we receive from others it is a reminder of how to be compassionate when we are in a position to strengthen our brother or sister the next time.

A month ago, I was at my father's house for a family function. It was a hot summer day, and the children were eager to get into the pool. Their ages range from months old to early teens. Multiple times the adults reprimanded the younger children to stay on the shallow end if they were not wearing life jackets. We knew they couldn't swim as well as they thought. A couple of times, we found a child drifting towards the deep end that is at least nine feet deep. There were multiple children and adults in and around the pool for hours. I was standing by the patio table taking a break when I heard my son, Judah, screaming for help. I looked up quickly to see he was at the far end of the pool with two other little cousins who weren't supposed to be there. I think they held onto the side of the pool and made their way back, or maybe they went on the steps in the deep end. Either way, he was too far from the steps or side. He began to realize he was not as good at swimming as he thought. I immediately began running to the other end of the pool, yelling for the other cousins to reach out and grab his hand. They were scared frozen, just looking. As I'm running to the deep end, I'm praying that he is close enough for me to grab without

F. Y. I.

having to jump in fully. I can swim, but I have a phobia of drowning. I do not go into the water if I cannot stand up. I was quickly facing a decision to jump in and grab him while being afraid for my own safety. As a mother, I decided I would get to him and throw him towards the steps where he could stand up and figure the rest out once I got in there.

All the time, Judah was screaming, "Help!" He began crying and was fighting his hardest to stay above the water. He would go down and quickly kick and fight with all his might to get back up. This seemed as if time was moving in slow motion, but in real-time, it was probably less than a minute from beginning to end. I stepped down the stairs and snatched him out. Everyone's emotions were very high at the moment. I reprimanded him and made him change clothes because he was done swimming that day. Then, I hugged him tight and explained why it was so important to listen to instructions. Above all of that, I'm grateful that he yelled for help when he did. He and his cousins were being sneaky the whole time getting to the deep end. Had he tried to conceal his disobedience any longer, this story could have ended in tragedy. He couldn't worry about whether he was going to get in trouble or not at that moment. It was life and death.

In life, we can be like these children. Sometimes we are headed into the deep end but don't know we cannot swim. We have asked to go into positions and places that we really don't know how to handle. It is better to ask for help! Use your voice and scream "HELP!". Pay attention to the people around you who seem as if they are out of control with their anger, rage, frustration, or aggressive verbal attacks on others. These are often people in enormous pain who need help but don't know how or who to ask. Also, look out for those who have completely

F. Y. I.

withdrawn because they could be on the verge of taking their own lives. Not everyone who is depressed or suicidal suffers for long periods before taking action. We all need one another.

One of my favorite sayings as a young soldier to my friends was, "Cover me while I move!" The proper response is "Covered!" or "I got you covered!" This is the ultimate illustration of teamwork. We are all trying to make it safely through the battlefield of life, but to do so, we need some battle buddies or life buddies. We need someone who can lay down suppressive fire while we're running forward towards the goal. In other words, we need someone who can send up some powerful prayers, strengthening words, acts of kindness, etc. while we're pushing forward.

It's not only time for you to use your voice, but it's time for you to start running forward! I got you covered buddy. It's time to move!

F. Y. I.

Chapter Seven

During the Pain

I wrote and published my first book in 2015, entitled *After the Pain: Transforming Pain into Personal Power*. If you haven't read that one, I encourage you to get a copy after you finish this. In that book, I took the time to go step by step through the process of embracing the hardships of life and using them all for your ultimate benefit. As I was preparing this project, I thought "I've given the tools for after the pain. But what in the world are we supposed to do during the pain?" I wrestled with where even to put this in the book because it's such a critical piece of thriving in our lives.

Types of Pain

There are different types of pain, and that determines how we can handle the pain. Anticipated pain is the pain you know is coming and can begin preparing for mentally and emotionally. This pain may be with the potential loss of a loved one with a terminal illness. This can be the pain of going through a break-up or divorce.

F. Y. I.

This can be the pain of moving away from the people you love. You know it's coming even if you don't know exactly when. You are bracing yourself for it. Then, there is unexpected pain. This pain catches you off guard. This pain is like that phone call that you've lost a loved one in a tragic accident or crime. It's the moment you get a photo of your spouse committing adultery. It's the moment the doctor tells you your test results show a chronic disease you did not think you were even at risk to carry. It's the heart attack that catches you while walking in the mall. It's abrasive and intrusive, and it can place you in a whirlwind of emotions. It's like walking down a sunny street, and then suddenly it starts thundering, lightning, and pouring down rain. Whether anticipated or unexpected, you are faced with the choice to deal with the pain or avoid it. Sometimes, we do not have to capacity to face the pain head-on when it first hits, but be certain the pain won't leave until it has been acknowledged, addressed, and properly processed.

There is also acute pain. Acute pain is discomfort with a time limit. It's temporary. You know it has a definite endpoint even if you don't know when that is. You can encourage yourself during this pain with phrases such as "This too shall pass." "It won't always be this way." "Seasons must change." "Weeping may endure for a night, but joy comes in the morning[19]." In the most intense moments of pain and anguish, you are strengthened to endure because you know there's relief coming. This pain can be like an injury during exercise. Whether a sprain or fracture, it's going to heal in weeks to months with proper care. In life, this can be like losing a job. It can be a disagreement with a close friend or family member. It can be the experience of betrayal or disappointment. It's in the

F. Y. I.

moments you were looked over for the promotion. It's in the situations that open the well of your emotions.

If acute pain is unaddressed, mismanaged, or disregarded, it can progress into chronic pain. This pain is more taxing mentally because you cannot see an end. This can be a diagnosis of a life-long illness. This can be a disagreement that turned into a grudge that progressed into a huge rift in the relationship with no signs of reconciliation. This can be learning to live again after losing a loved one. This can be watching someone you love slowly deteriorate. It's a pain that you face on a regular basis. Either every day, week, month, or several months. Even when you have good days, you know it's coming back. It's a pain that lasts for months and years. It's a pain you must learn how to deal with. There is no cure to it. There are only management options. This type of pain wears on the soul of mankind. It's like the continued state of injustice, prejudice, discrimination, the seemingly insurmountable mountain of hatred before our society. We try to treat it, to cure it, to expose it and to defeat it, yet we see it surface in different platforms and vicinities. It's like cancer that has metastasized all over the world. How do we kill the disease without killing the people?

It's the child growing up in an abusive home. It's the residual effects of anyone who's suffered emotional, mental, physical, or sexual abuse. It's the pain of a parent who's buried a child. It's the pain of the parents who miscarried and never got to hold their child alive. It's the pain of the child who was abandoned by a parent or both parents, left wondering why they weren't enough or what they did wrong. It's the pain of the war veteran who's seen things they cannot repeat because of the sensitivity of

F. Y. I.

security. It's the men and women suffering from post-traumatic stress disorder. It's the parents of a child born disabled. It's the state many are living in or, at least, trying to live through.

There are situational pains. There are voluntary pains. There are necessary pains. Necessary pains are often the times when we need a warning or a change in direction. I have experienced necessary pains when I did not want to let go of my will, but GOD knew destruction was ahead. It's the moments of chastisement and correction. It's the moments we are caught in error and have to pay the consequences for our decisions. It's the moments of failure when we did not properly prepare. It's the moments of isolation required to align our souls back to our purpose. It's the moments I have to tell my children "no" because they don't understand the magnitude of what they're asking for or doing. It's the pivotal point where we enter the crossroads of life and need a nudge in the right direction. Necessary pains are the ones where we realize afterward that it was good for us to be afflicted[20]. The affliction was our protection. The affliction was our teacher. The affliction was our clarity. The affliction was your defining moment.

There's also a pain I am learning to master. It's productive pain. Productive pain is the discomfort caused when intentionally becoming stronger. It's the time I spend in the gym pushing my body while I'm out of breath, sweating, and growing tired. It's the pain I feel for two to three days after the workout where I'm sore all over. That pain produces the muscle tone and strength I'm intentionally striving to achieve. In life, it's the late nights studying or working on your dream. It's the sacrifice of

F. Y. I.

time and social pleasures while advancing your career. It's the money you give up ensuring you spend the quality time with your family so you don't lose them. It's the time you spend being ridiculed for your dream because the moment you succeed everyone's comments will change. It's the opposition that fuels your ambition even more.

There are so many types of pain that I cannot list them all. No matter what type of pain you are facing, or will face, take courage in the fact dead people don't feel pain. The fact you have pain is an indication that you are ALIVE! You may wish you were dead at times because the pain is unbearable. I know because I have been there. I have had patients in so much pain they asked if we could just cut off the body part causing the discomfort. They were willing to lose body parts because the pain of having the pain was more than they could tolerate. I have been like those patients in the course of life. I have had painful areas that I just wanted to cut them completely off. Amputation, sometimes, seems like the best option but it is often the last option in most cases. Amputation does not guarantee a complete resolution of pain. In fact, many patients who have physical amputations have phantom pain. This offers after a body part is removed. The patient's foot hurts, but they have no foot. Their body remembers the pain their foot experienced before it was removed. Therefore, don't choose amputation under the false pretense it will take away all your pain. Not only is phantom pain real, but the pain of learning how to live without a vital component of who you are is a life-long challenge for amputees. Prosthetics have made life after amputation far better for amputees. Yet, each patient will tell you there was a strong

F. Y. I.

period of facing a hurdle to regaining functionality. It's work no matter which route you choose.

The Experience of Pain

I often experience how life works by learning how the physical body works. When we physically encounter pain, there are multiple signals involved. You do not actually experience pain at the site of injury. You experience pain once the nerve endings send the signal up the spinal cord to your brain for processing. The brain sends a signal back to the affected part of the body. Without the nerves, pain is not possible, but the injury is and the damage is possible. Pain, however, requires the nerves. For example, first and second-degree burns are very painful. The first two layers of skin are affected. By the time you reach third, and fourth-degree burns, the nerve endings are completely destroyed, and while it is the worst kind of burn, it is the least painful.

Without the nerves, pain is not possible. Nerves are the vital messengers between the physical occurrences and the perceived experiences.

Nerves are the messengers between the body and the brain. I venture to say that your nerves are the messengers between your experiences and your mind. I wondered where the phrase, "You're getting on my nerves" or "You're getting on my last nerve!" came originated. The significance of this statement is that we use it in the context

F. Y. I.

of referring to emotional annoyance, frustration, agitation, and distress. We use phrases like "my nerves are bad" to describe our anxieties.

Pain Management

Physical pain management is achieved through various forms of medications. Local anesthetics block the nerve signals from leaving the location, so you never experience the pain, although trauma or painful stimuli are still occurring. With local anesthesia, you are still awake and aware of what's taking place. You are simply not experiencing physical pain. General anesthesia also blocks nerve signals between the brain and body, but it also prevents you from remembering any part of the procedure. I've received two epidurals during childbirth, and I could not feel anything from my stomach downward. This is a form of regional anesthesia. I could feel the babies coming out, but it was not a painful stimulation. It simply felt like pressure. I've experienced local anesthesia at the dentist's office. The initial injection burned, then afterward, I didn't feel pain only pressure. Last, I experienced general anesthesia for a surgical procedure. I remember lying on the operating table, and the anesthesiologist telling some jokes he thought were hilarious, even though I did not think they were funny. He told me to start counting, and all I remember is waking up in the recovery room. I couldn't tell you what happened while I was asleep. I woke up, and my surgery was complete. I had the surgical bandage there to prove it. It wasn't until the anesthesia wore completely off that I began feeling any pain.

F. Y. I.

Just like I have utilized these forms of pain management during intense physical conditions, I have tried to use these with emotional pain. I have tried the local anesthesia approach for the particular relationship or event that hurt. The agent I used often was anger. Anger feels better than hurt. Therefore, I held on to every memory that enraged me, so I could avoid the sobering feeling of being hurt and disappointed. Whenever I wanted to cry or began feeling the pain, I would find a way back to anger to numb the pain. You, however, may achieve this with the unforgiveness of the person who hurt you the worse. Some get their local anesthesia by ruining that person's reputation or publicly bashing them. Some get it by being vindictive and getting revenge. No matter how you get revenge, just know it's only temporary relief. It does not remove the injury; it only shields you from feeling or acknowledging it.

When the source of pain in life came from multiple sources at once, I would look for the epidural or regional anesthesia. I needed to be awake to handle my other responsibilities, but I didn't want to feel anything from the heart down. This is the period where I would intellectually analyze every situation and justify why I didn't deserve the painful experience. I would develop a tunnel vision on one or two areas of life that were still bringing me joy. I know I'm not the only one who has done this. Therefore, if work is the most peaceful place you have, then longer hours start to pile up at work voluntarily, or if the children are the only source of consistent relief, then overcompensation and splurging may take place. You begin living through the children's gifts or talents. If they're good in gymnastics; your entire focus is on gymnastics. If it's performing arts, sports, or academics, that's where you engulf yourself.

F. Y. I.

Then there are times where I wanted to check out completely. For me, this was when depression had its free course with me. I was completely numb. I was in the room, but my mind was somewhere else. I was going through the motions, but I was completely checked out because the pain was too much to process. I was looking for general anesthesia, and to be completely honest, there were times when I have prayed to the FATHER, *"Please take this cup from me. Hide me in YOUR shadow. Take me out of this place.*[21]*"* There were times when GOD sustained me from completely having a mental breakdown by giving me access to HIS presence. Worship is certainly an experience where I've gotten lost in prayer. I couldn't tell you what happened between the time I entered and left, but I left knowing the work was done.

As good as anesthesia is, we cannot live under anesthesia. Eventually, we will feel again.

What do we do when we have to go through the pain? How do we manage it? Surely, life is bound to bring some uncomfortable places.

B.R.E.A.T.H.E.

Breathe, Refocus, Exercise, Adjust, Thanksgiving, Hope, & Embrace

𝓕. 𝒴. 𝐼.

Breathe

No matter what the source of pain is, you have to keep breathing. Breath is a representation of life itself. The ability to breathe is the difference between life and death. The true purpose of breathing is to provide the body with oxygen because every tissue in your body needs oxygen to survive. In fact, the lack of oxygen in tissue is a direct cause of pain. Oxygen is required to produce energy by breaking down the sugar and fatty acids in your body. This is why the lack of oxygen quickly leads to unconsciousness. While performing procedures in clinic, we remind patients to take slow deep breaths to calm them. It helps to distract them. It helps to keep them from becoming anxious and to keep them from passing out by the vagal reflex.

Some trials in life will literally take your breath away and it can make it hard to catch your breath. You should first stop and breathe through the pain and inhale the good in your life. One of the biggest problems with being in pain is we forget how many other areas of our body or life are still healthy. You CANNOT give up on living because you are in pain. Slow down. Be deliberate in what you give your energy to. Conserve your strength. With every inhalation, remember you are one breath closer to the end of this trial. With every exhalation, release the anxiety, stress, toxicity, worry, complaints, and thought that this will never end. Breathe in LIFE! Fill your space with positivity, peace, and power. You have to remember to keep doing what gives you life, inspiration, encouragement, confidence, pleasure, etc. when you're going through pain. Most times, we hold our breath and vagal down or pass out. Friend, please don't stop breathing. There is still joy

F. Y. I.

available to you. There is still peace available to you. There is still hope available to you. Just take it in.

Refocus

Do not focus on the pain, focus on the process.

One of the pitfalls in the midst of life's tumultuous storms is focusing on the wrong area. The quickest way to drown is to focus on the water and not swimming to shore. The water is not going anywhere. It's not supposed to. You, on the other hand, need to get moving to safety. You can complain about whose fault it is that you're about to drown. You can sit there pointing fingers at the people watching you drown. You can run the list of reasons why you don't deserve to be in the place that you're in. You can look at the storm like Peter[22] and begin to sink, or you can look to the SOURCE and cry "HELP ME!" No parent willingly lets his or her child drown. Ask your FATHER to help you. Ask your family to help you.

Whether physical, emotional, mental, or spiritual pain, when I learned to focus on the process, the pain became bearable. In the midst of childbirth labor, when I focused on pushing the baby out, the pain was just fuel to push harder.

When you cannot eliminate the pain, you must learn to use it as your motivation to push harder.

F. Y. I.

Pain can cause you to pray harder than you've ever prayed. Pain can cause you to have faith more than you ever have. Pain can cause you to find a strength that you never knew you had. If you focus on the present, your painful experience will last much longer than it should. The nerves are the messengers of pain to the brain. Therefore, focus is the tool to block the signal.

You may experience the pressure, but you don't have to continue feeling the pain.

The events don't have to stop for the pain to stop. Your perception of life's situations dictates whether you call it pain, or whether you call it pressure to move forward. Whatever it is you're experiencing, ALWAYS take a moment to fix your focus!

Exercise

Research shows that physical exercise is a great source of mental pain relief. The chemicals produced in our brains with pleasurable activities help create a favorable balance that produces good feelings. Not only is exercise good for your physical health, but it is also good for your mental health. As I have shared before, weight training in the CrossFit gym definitely stretches me past where I think I can go. More times than not, I shortchanged myself versus overextending myself. I love to run. I have been doing it for

F. Y. I.

most of my life. There's something about running that allows me to tunnel my frustrations and burn them out on the course. The more hurt I feel in my emotions, the harder I run. By the end of the run, I have shifted the pain from my mind to my feet. It feels good because once again, I have used my pain as fuel to improve my body, health, and ultimately life.

I definitely encourage you to do some physical exercise. Maybe, you enjoy dancing and not going to the gym. Maybe, you enjoy walking. Whether it's sports or cutting grass, get your body moving. Exercise is not just for the physical activity. I want you to exercise your faith! Many of us would not have any faith had we not endured some hardships in this life. I can be completely honest with you. My faith wouldn't have the power or strength it does if it were not for the many opportunities to exercise it.

Faith is the confidence that impossible things don't exist. Everything becomes possible with faith.

The longer you live with limitations placed on yourself, your career, or your life, the more your faith needs development. I believe there are strategic trials in life that target a specific muscle group in your faith. If you want to survive not only the pain but thrive through the pain, you must also exercise your faith. Speak life until you see life! Speak blessings until blessings manifest. Speak strength until strength comes. Speak joy until joy overtakes you. Speak light until life gets as bright as the sun for you. Exercise your faith!

You may not know how to speak to the mountain in the beginning[23]. You may have to start by speaking to the

F. Y. I.

ant hill. Once your faith blows the ant hill away, then speak to the fig tree. Once the fig tree dries up, speak to the waters. Once the waters part, speak to the mountain! Build your faith!

I didn't know how to have faith for the great requests. I started believing for "small" requests. I had faith I could sit on a chair, and it wouldn't break. You have that faith too. You exercise it every time you sit down. I had faith I would wake up when my alarm went off in the morning. You have that faith too. You wake up every morning, and you're not surprised or shocked that your eyes opened. In fact, you expect it without conscious thought. I began having faith I would arrive safely at my destination when I left my house. You have that faith too. You get in your car, or on the bus, train, plane and get where you want to go. I began having faith that I would get paid on my designated payday. You have that faith too. You plan your spending based on the fact your pay is coming. I began having faith for *bigger* moments.

I am writing this book with the faith that someone will buy and read it. And guess what? You're reading it right now as a result of my faith. You're also reading as a result of your faith that you would find something significant and applicable to your life between the covers of the book.

Then, I had to believe for even greater moments. I had faith my body would be healed. When the doctors couldn't tell me what was wrong with me, the HEALER stepped in and did what medicine couldn't. You cannot convince me that healing isn't possible because I have experienced it for myself. I also had to believe that I could break the bonds of poverty off my life and live in a place of more than enough. I had to endure seeing the negative balances in my account and asking for extensions on bills, but with discipline and education, I learned how to live within my means and experience more than enough

F. Y. I.

between paydays. I went from barely giving five and ten dollars in tithes to years with giving five figures in charitable donations. I had faith that if I was faithful over the few dollars I had, I would be made the ruler of many dollars[24]. I had faith that if I was willing to sow into the lives of others, that I would always have seed to sow. I had faith that I could be loved for who I truly was, flaws and all. I had faith that I was enough, in fact, more than enough. That faith produced love from people I have not ever met physically, but have touched in a positive way.

I had faith that a child from the drug and crime-infested streets of South Philadelphia could one day be called Dr. LaChish without ever inhaling, ingesting, or injecting one drug into my body. I had faith I would never live behind bars. I had faith I didn't have to rob, cheat, or bribe my way to success. I had faith that integrity would be my badge of honor, and elevation would come in due season. I had faith that no trial would be wasted in my life. I had faith every ounce of rock thrown my way would be a stepping stone for me to climb higher heights. I had faith that every promise made to me by the ALMIGHTY would come to pass. I am exercising my faith daily. Exercise yours!

<u>Adjust Your Load</u>

I was going to work each day taking my backpack with me, carrying my computer, my tools for class or clinic, and my food. I began noticing my bag was getting really heavy. My shoulders were actually hurting one day walking into work. The next morning before I got out of the car, I stopped for a second to look into my bag. I didn't know what was making it so heavy. As I looked through each compartment, I realized I had been adding items to the bag, but not taking anything out when I didn't need it. I had

F. Y. I.

multiple bottles of water. I had books I wasn't using. I had trash and snacks I forgot were in there. I began emptying everything I didn't need for work that day out of the bag. By the time I got out of the car, my bag was much lighter. How often have I carried unnecessary weight around in life because I never took the time to adjust my load?

Sometimes, the source of pain in your life is due to your failure to adjust the load. You have to empty the trash you've been carrying around in your heart, mind, and spirit. You have to take out the knowledge you used in past experiences that do not apply now. You have to assess when you have more than what you need and get rid of the excess. Your shoulders can carry the load designed for you, but you'll hurt your back trying to carry more than you can bear. Learn how to cast your cares on the ONE who has All-Power[25]. Stop trying to be a superhero and run your own race in life. Overextending yourself is a preventable pain. Sometimes, we carry other people's burdens for them, instead of with them. Stop allowing people to use you when you're already full to capacity. Point them to the SOURCE and let them choose to cast their cares to HIM.

I'm so grateful the burdens I've been designated are light, and the yoke is easy[26]. This simply means the things in my power and job description are all within my scope of practice. Once I start trying to carry, fix, and mend everything, it's time to refer to HIM. If your load is too heavy right now friend, take a moment to give it to the ONE who is able.

𝓕. 𝒴. 𝐼.

Thanksgiving

An attitude of gratitude makes all the difference.

Nothing has shifted my pain as strongly as stopping to be thankful in the middle of my problems — your focus matters. Your attitude matters even more. I remind myself in my darkest hours that I still have so much to be grateful for. For example, I found myself diagnosed with viral meningitis while I was seven months pregnant with Zion. I had been having a persistent headache over the course of three days or so before being diagnosed. The first time I went to the emergency room, the doctor treated me for a migraine. The medicine relieved my pain at the moment, but after I went home, and within a couple of hours I was right back in extreme pain. It was the worse headache of my life. Then, the second time I went to the emergency room they did a spinal tap and CT scan of my brain. They immediately came back with masks on, explaining I would be admitted and not going home. This was my first time being kept in the hospital overnight for an illness. I spent four nights in the hospital that week. I had no family in the area, and my son Judah had to stay with a church member. In fact, I didn't even call my family to tell them I was in the hospital because I didn't want to stress them out from twelve hours away. I also could not bear even looking at the phone screen because I was in so much pain. I was scared for the health of my unborn child because I didn't know if he would be infected or affected.

F. Y. I.

I believe it was the second night of multiple antibiotics and antivirals, and pain that was relieved only by the strongest narcotic where I began to think. The next morning, the doctors came in and told me I did not have the life-threatening strain, and the baby was not affected at all. When they left the room, I began to thank GOD that I had another testimony. I experienced HIM in a whole new light that week. I had experienced illnesses before, and healing, but this time was different. I was literally disabled by the pain, and no position was comfortable. Not only did HE keep me, but HE kept my baby healthy as well. I began to thank GOD and the people who stepped up to help me with everything.

I promise if you start making a list of everything you are thankful for, the pain will lose its intensity. There is a lifting that occurs in thankfulness that is indescribable. Complaining only compounds the pain. Stop and say, "Thank you!" right now. Be thankful for your life, no matter how difficult it is right now.

At the age of sixteen, I went to Kenya for a mission trip. During that trip, I spent the night in an orphanage with my sister and two other friends. I was able to work with the physician we came to support. I witnessed children with no possessions of their own who were singing, dancing, serving, and celebrating over our presence. I was able to rub medication over the body of a little child with scabies. There was no part of his little body that had not been plagued with rashes, itching, discomfort. I will never forget him. After I finished putting the medicine, he looked up and said "Thank you" in Swahili, "Asante." It brings tears to my eyes, reflecting on that moment because in my mind, I didn't deserve a thank you since he didn't have much to be thankful for. He was poor. He was abandoned by his family. He was sleeping on a mattress infested with bugs. He was living in an orphanage with the only clothes and toys he had based on donation. He deserved my pity. Instead, he taught me a lesson that would change my life forever. I should spend less time counting what I don't have, and more time showing gratitude for what I do have.

He thanked me because I took a moment to help him feel a little better physically. I wasn't scared to touch him. I wasn't worried about whether he would give scabies to me. I wanted him to heal. I wanted him to experience the standard of living I had taken for granted up until that point. I was honored to serve him. I was honored to serve all of the people I met during that trip. I realized that on my worst day, there are millions of people who would trade places with me gladly. His "Thank you" was unexpected, but it made me want to do more because he appreciated the small thing I could do. His gratitude unlocked his blessing. Friend, perhaps your pain is persisting because you are withholding the key to your blessing.

Worship works miracles in a matter of moments.

Hope Against Hope

Maintaining your hope is imperative to your mental capacity to handle life's difficulties. The moment all hope is lost, people give up. If all hope is lost in the relationship, we often give up. If all hope is lost on the career path, we might give up. If all hope is lost on a cure, we might give

F. Y. I.

up. If all hope is lost in life, we might give up. Everyone who has attempted or committed suicide reached a point where he or she had no hope for life to improve.

Hope is the heartbeat of faith.

Abraham is considered the Father of Faith. He is esteemed for hoping against hope for the promise to come to pass[27]. He had every reason NOT to believe. Despite all the facts against him, he still believed until he received the promise.

Some of you may be crushed by the pain because you have no hope. I can honestly understand. There may not be a cure for that condition. There is no way to bring loved ones back from the dead. There may not be an easy way out of all the debt you've accumulated. There may be insurmountable odds against you. The facts are very discouraging, but I'm glad I live a life like Abraham with hope despite the facts.

I hope for outcomes that science says is impossible. With all of my education and professionalism, my hope is built on the SOLID ROCK. When your only source is you and other humans, you live with a constant disadvantage. You are confined to the knowledge and ability of mankind. However, when you tap into an everlasting source, you can say with assurance that nothing shall be impossible because I believe[28]!

Friend, I know you may have many reasons to cancel hope. You may have even experienced times when

F. Y. I.

hoping did not change the outcome, but you should not give up!

The key for my hope is my confidence that <u>it can happen</u>. I don't know if it will happen, but I believe that it can happen for me.

Even if it doesn't happen, my hope was not wasted. The pressure was not on me to perform the miracle. That's a burden I am not strong enough to carry. As long as you are living there is a reason to hope for better.

When I was a child, I sang in the junior choir at my church. There was one particular song that I lead for many years until I graduated. Even the times I went back to visit I would be invited to sing it again. The song's lyrics talked about hope. "There is hope, yes there is hope[29]." The song spoke of the violence in schools, the heartaches of the world, and all the sources of despair. After listing all of the reasons to be despondent, it came back to remind us "There is hope!" I know you have moments where the list of reasons to stop believing are longer than the reasons to believe. It doesn't matter how long either list is. What matters is there is at one reason on the list to hope. I'm here to remind you that the greatest people to live who achieved their goals and became legends for ages to come are these individuals who dared to believe their hope would be fulfilled if they persevered.

ℱ. 𝒴. ℐ.

Embrace

My last point is to take a moment to embrace the experience you're in. Learn as much as you can while you're going through it. Learn the lesson the first time, so you don't have to try again. When you reach those moments where you cannot change the pain, embrace the opportunity to become wiser. Embrace the opportunity to become a demonstrator. Embrace the opportunity to become a teacher and a source of hope for others who are watching you go through your pain.

I try my best to find the most positive perspective of any situation. I don't always understand the process or purpose, but I embrace the opportunity to become more of who I was created to be. For example, a piece of clay is valueless until it finishes its process in the potter's hands. I don't know the limits or extents of my purpose in this world, but I embrace the fact it's bigger than I am.

Embracing the pain does not mean approving it or enjoying it. Embracing means you make peace with its existence. Embracing means you force it to make peace with your existence. You are a worthy opponent to every obstacle life gives you. You are living in a story designed before the foundations of the world. The end of your story has already been written in stone. You are the star of this story. You are like Rocky Balboa[30]. It doesn't matter how bad your opponent is beating you round after round, you eventually will win! Raise your hands as a sign of victory. Embrace the plot of your victorious ending. You don't have to be the favorite going in to win. When the writer is your FATHER, you have no other choice but to win.

F. Y. I.

B.R.E.A.T.H.E.

Keep breathing. Refocus on the process, not the pain. Exercise your faith. Adjust your load and remove every excess weight. Take a moment to be thankful. Hope against the odds. Embrace the experience as a testimony that offers you the opportunity to earn your title, More Than a Conqueror.

Dear Friend, learn how to B.R.E.A.T.H.E. during pain. The pain doesn't ever kill you. It may make you want to die, but it's not the pain that kills you. Pain is a subjective experience. You make of it what you will. Always remember that when you cannot manage the pain on your own, seek professional help. There is no shame in saving your life.

I would be remiss if I didn't tell you that I have had to take moments to go into the psychologist's office and work through some pain. I have been in the psychiatrist's office as he prescribed medication to help me regain my drive to get out of bed in the morning. I have been to the counselor more than once. I have been in the prayer line more than once. Untreated depression can literally create an imbalance in your brain that takes your cognitive function away. A mental breakdown does not only occur in "weak-minded" people. Behavioral health is not just for "crazy" people. Unexpected and chronic pain are the most life-threatening pains for the human psyche. Imagine being hit by a freight train while driving a car. No one would expect you to get out of the car, brush it off, and walk away unphased. Even if you are not physically aware of your injuries, before you are cleared to try to walk, the emergency room has to rule out life-threatening injuries.

F. Y. I.

Likewise, there are experiences in life that we are just not prepared for. Before you tell yourself to brush it off, make sure you are truly healthy. It's hard to walk on broken bones. It's even harder to live with a broken spirit.

You can survive any pain. I want you to thrive, not just survive.

F. Y. I.

Chapter Eight

FREE YOURSELF

The term freedom has varying levels of depth to various groups of people. For individuals with no history of bondage or residual effects of former enslavement, this word can be a source of inspiration and casually uplifting. However, for those who have experienced personal bondage, incarceration, entrapment, enslavement, oppression, depression, or suppression, the word freedom provokes a deep-rooted desire, craving, and cry for restoration to a place where they were denied.

> Webster defines freedom as "1: the quality or state of being free: as. a: the absence of necessity, coercion, or constraint in choice or action. b: liberation from slavery or restraint or from the power of another. c: the quality or state of being exempt or released from something onerous."

Of course, we have to visit the root word to gain a greater understanding. Webster has many definitions of "free" since it can be a noun, verb, or adjective. I'll just share a couple that are most relevant to the freedom I am seeking for and with you.

Free: not subject to the control or domination of another; not determined by anything beyond its own nature of being; choosing or capable of choosing for itself; not bound, confined, or detained by force.

𝓕. 𝒴. 𝐼.

In order for you to appreciate this chapter, you must first identify your limitations, confinement, restraints, strongholds, prisons, and points of contention. You are likely a slave, but your master is so clever that it has you thinking you're in control. Now, I understand history, and in the United States slavery ended hundreds of years ago. The physical ability of one human to own another human was abolished. However, the mental ability of one human to own another is still very prevalent. Let's clarify further.

A slave is a person who does not carry the highest influence in his or her life.

The decisions made are not independent, but greatly reflect another's desire to be more dominant. A slave is required to live where another dictates. A slave is required to eat and drink what another determines. A slave must come and go when another commands. A slave must cater to the master and is subject to suffering when the master is not satisfied. A slave is obligated to fulfilling the master's agenda, whether it is contrary to the slave's personal desires or not. A slave is not in control of his or her thoughts, emotions, conduct, or life vision. A slave is confined to exist within the parameters set by an external influence who has defined what the identity of the slave can be. A slave is confined to dream within the box set before them. A slave is confined to be who the master wants the slave to be.

A slave is a human who has been robbed of his or her GOD given purpose, light, and hope.

F. Y. I.

Have you been a slave? Of course not! We may emphatically declare that we are not; however, there is a chance that we could be slaves. For example, are you currently holding unforgiveness in your heart towards someone who hurt you in the past? If so, you are enslaved to the situation that infected your heart. You're confined to living within the parameters unforgiveness has set for you. Are you currently or have you been bothered by the mention of someone's name? Does your mood shift when you hear that name or see that person's face in a photo or video? Does it cause you to roll your eyes automatically? Sigh? Take a deep breath? Mumble choice words under your breath? Shut down? Does the mention of that person's name, sight of his or her face, or energy of his or her presence send you on an emotional trip that ends you in a lower state than you were? If so, you are ensnared in your emotions by another person's existence. Your emotional stability and frequency are controlled by the absence or presence of that individual's energy. It carries an overwhelming burden, and that reflects bondage.

When you evaluate the goals you have not accomplished yet, do you have someone or something you attribute that to? Do you regret ever connecting with certain people? Do you use comments such as, "My life would've been so much better if I never would've hooked up with them?" Or, "Ever since they came into my life, everything has been going down?" Or, "I have bad luck because my family is a mess?"

Do you blame other people for your unhappiness? Do you blame other people for your dissatisfaction in life? Do you blame other people for anything negative you feel? If so, you are making yourself a slave to whomever you're using as the identified reason why your life is not what you want it to be. The trouble with this type of slavery is

F. Y. I.

sometimes the person you have made your master doesn't even know it. Sometimes, we harbor secrets in our hearts towards people who don't even know we are still hurt, bothered, tormented, or affected by something they said, did, or neglected to say or do. In addition, while you think you are holding them accountable for their actions by not letting it go, you are truly holding yourself hostage to a place in your past that limits your ability to advance in your present.

Let me remind you that your life is not designed to be managed by anyone else. You and GOD are the two entities in charge of getting you to your destination. GOD's role is to direct your path down every necessary road that will equip you to occupy your destined purpose and platform. GOD is there as a SOURCE to fulfill every need you experience along the journey. HE has everything required in stock, and HE never runs out. Therefore, when you are lacking joy, peace, love, comfort, security, confidence, clarity, courage, etc. you must plug back into the SOURCE. GOD is your Source, and yet HE has placed the well within you to pull from. When you think you are lacking something, GOD will often place you in situations where you have to search for your solutions. You are an earthen treasure[32], and there is so much planted in your soul and spirit that you haven't even uncovered. While you are seeking all of these outcomes from someone else, GOD has placed the fulfillment for every desire you could have already within you. When you are blessed to find another human being that "provides" positive emotions and energy to you, it is really that person assisting you in discovering what was in you all along.

GOD has a role, and HE fulfills it. You also have a role, and this is where many of us have struggled. I'm not sure if this is something we were taught or if it's something

F. Y. I.

that we assumed, but other people are not responsible for our emotional well-being. Allow me to burst a few myths that I was deceived by in my journey.

1. My parents' job was not to give me everything I wanted so I could be happy.

The job of a parent is to equip each child to his or her maximum capacity so the child can face life responsibly and expand his or her own capacity while fulfilling a purpose. My parent's job was to pull the tension back so far on the arrow that when it was released, I could go as far as possible in my purpose. How good I rate their parenting is not the determining factor for whether I am successful or not. Of course, I did not learn this truth until I became a parent myself. I thank GOD for my parents and all the many lessons they continue to teach me directly and indirectly.

There are many adults who are holding grudges against their parents. The generation of today has such a sense of entitlement that they can be impossible to please. Some complain their parents were too strict and overbearing. Others will complain their parents were too emotionally detached and did not provide enough guidance. As I parent my children, I am eerily aware that parenting is one of the most complex jobs a human could ever have. Having multiple children does not make it any easier because each child is an individual. The approach is not blanketed or should not be across every child. I have children with varying levels of sensitivity. One child, I can discipline and penetrate with a simple look of disappointment. Two of my children require a more intense interaction to break their negative behaviors. What I have learned in

F. Y. I.

moments where I felt I was not communicating effectively is that my children have a great level of influence on one another. Their sense of belonging to one another's team is very significant for them. Sibling love instills a sense of wanting to be better for one another. There are moments a big sister or brother talk can be more effective than a mom or dad talk. It doesn't make me a bad parent to leverage that.

All in all, take time to consider what kind of parenting your parents provided for you. Then, consider what kind of parenting they received, and know with the assurance your grandparents treat you much better than they treated your parents. Therefore, take that into consideration when calculating how equipped your parents were for you. Also, realize you are a unique individual who did not come with a user manual. You are evolving in knowing yourself. Extend grace to your parents for trying to keep up with your evolution from an infant until now.

2. **My children or dependents cannot be my foundational source of worth in this world.**

Good parents have a burning desire to do everything in their power to provide the best life possible for their children. Whatever the definition of "best" is for that person becomes the driving force and heaviest influence for every decision they make from the time the child is born until the child becomes an independent adult. Becoming parents can make people change their entire career track, savings plans, retirement age goals, etc. We make comments such as, "my kids are my everything." I truly understand this sentiment. Nevertheless, it is critically important to maintain your

F. Y. I.

own identity and internal source of life's greatest emotions because children grow up and leave. When they leave, many parents who have made their babies their everything are left with nothing but emptiness and a huge void. Empty nester syndrome is real. You can spend 18+ years of your adult life trying to make perfect decisions for your child's well-being, and once they are out of your home, you don't know how to make decisions for your well-being. In fact, you may not even know who you are anymore outside of "mom" or "dad." Therefore, you may rush them to have children, so you can have grandchildren, and they become your new everything. The problem with that is grandchildren become adults one day too and may not want to spend time with you anymore, so then who are you? Where is your everything then?

You cannot make your entire existence and value dependent upon someone needing you.

3. **Your spouse, or lack of spouse, does not determine your completeness.**

I am a relationship person. I have always been that way since I was a young child. I like to be in a relationship because I enjoy having someone special to share experiences with and conversations that are intimate. I am an affectionate person, so I enjoy the physical aspects of being in a romantic relationship as well. Keeping this in mind, you were not designed to be incomplete without a spouse. Whoever started the phrase "My husband/wife completes me," I'm sure had very good intentions and

F. Y. I.

meant it in the purest of ways. However, today we have turned it into a source of confinement for many.

Now, we have singles who feel as if it is a curse to be single and are desperately seeking a mate, so they can stop receiving the awkward questions about when they're getting married, having children, or what their sexual orientation is. Being single has become a mental battle against depression because society has misconstrued the context and purpose of relationships and marriage. People are walking around unfulfilled and incomplete because they haven't found Mr. or Mrs. Right. Let me free you from that lie!

You are a complete creation all by yourself! There is nothing ½ or ¼ about you that are waiting for a spouse and/or child to complete. If you are not 100% whole when you get married, you won't become 100% whole because you got married. In fact, often getting married exposes how much work you should have done on yourself before marriage. Your spouse or future spouse should complement you, not complete you. The spouse should enhance you, accessorize you, inspire and propel you with their love, support, and presence. You cannot require them to complete you because they didn't make you! That person does not know how to repair the original designer's intent. If you cannot identify your own sources of lack, he/she is ill-equipped to make you whole. This is not because he/she doesn't want to or shouldn't want to help you become an even better version of yourself than you've been. It is because he/she is a human just like you with his or her own mental, emotional, physical, and spiritual battles faced daily. He/she can only help you from a place of abundance and not lack. Therefore, he/she must first have an abundance.

F. Y. I.

Stop asking your spouse or future spouse to become GOD. NO ONE can fulfill HIS place in your life! Likewise, as a spouse, it is not your job to become your partner's everything either. Pray for your spouse, encourage, uplift, pour into, cover, love, and remain committed to him or her. In doing these things, you will complement his/her life and enhance it. Allow him/her to enjoy your presence. And if by chance you are single, realize that one is still a whole number.

4. You are not responsible to fix or avoid every mistake that was made in your bloodline.

This one is a strong source of contention for me. As a child, I had a keen sense of spiritual gifts and was blessed with insight beyond my numerical years. I began tracing the patterns in my bloodline. I looked at both sides of my family. I looked at the men and the women. I looked at the education levels. I looked at the age and situations surrounding when they first became parents. I looked at the marital status. I looked at the presence or absenteeism of mothers and fathers. I looked at the dysfunctional cover-ups and the obligations to hide the shame of the parents. I looked at many areas, and I decided that I would break many of the patterns I consider to be generational curses.

GOD has blessed me to do that in many areas of my life. For that, I am eternally humbled, honored, grateful, and in awe. If you looked at the background I come from; statistically, I should not be who I am today. I did not allow the limitations of my ancestors in their day to continue in my life. I did not use their status as an excuse to aim lower. I did not use their statistics to defeat or deflate my ambitions and goals. On the other side, trying to carry the weight of generations of chains is unhealthy! I spent so

F. Y. I.

much time trying to "not be" and "not do" the behaviors I attributed to the curse, that it became a prison until I finally understood my approach was all wrong.

GOD did not place me here to bear the sins of my forefathers. They had their lives to live and give account for. I have my own life to live and account for. I cannot change one action they took along their journey, and that is not my job. I can only focus on my journey and do my absolute best to show a strong example of how to beat the odds. Nothing I do any longer is an effort to right their wrongs, but rather to begin a new legacy and heritage for those who are living with me and those who will live beyond me.

I don't have to redeem the bloodline. It has already been redeemed!

I cannot undo all the injustices and experiences my bloodline has suffered. I can add to my children's lives in such a way that they carry on a new tradition that replaces the negative patterns with incredible ones. My ancestors made their decisions based on what they knew, what they had, and what they faced in their time. My circumstances are very different, and my mentality is as well. I am here to encourage my relatives that we all have been equipped with greatness. We just have to let it out.

You do not have to bear the weight of breaking every negative generational pattern in your family. Sometimes we hurt our children, working so hard to make sure they don't make the same choices others did before them. We focus so much on the action or behavior, but not on the emotion that provoked the behavior. If we do not address the seed, the

F. Y. I.

fruit will eventually appear again. Instead of trying to stop the end result, work on the triggers. If no one has ever sought a degree, find out why? Were they intimidated by higher education? Were/are they functional illiterates? Were there learning disabilities that were never identified and treated? Were they too poor to pay for it? Were they so poor that getting a job was more important than developing a career? What is the root? If you can trace that, then you can easily create a new path forward that cannot be reversed.

Friend, please don't live your life trying to right the wrong of anyone else. You are setting yourself up for a never-ending cycle, where you will eventually be depleted and never stop to celebrate your own success. We cannot measure ourselves by anyone else's life because we all have our own individual journeys. If you are the first in your family to achieve something, CONGRATULATIONS! However, don't do it because you feel obligated to be the first. Do it because you are pursuing and fulfilling your purpose and maximizing your potential.

Motives mean everything when it comes to fulfillment.

There is a flip side to this point because some people are in the opposite narrative. You come from a legacy where everyone met a certain mark in life, and you are pressuring yourself to meet and exceed that mark. This is something I'm very sensitive about for my children especially. Friend, just because there are generations in your bloodline of people who pursued a certain occupation, vocation, or calling does not mean you have to. You may feel obligated not to break the tradition, but if it is not in

F. Y. I.

your heart to follow that path, be true to who you are. GOD has given us all a special passion that burns deeply within our souls.

Never dampen your fire out of duty or fear that you will cause another's fire to be extinguished.

The beauty of life is that we are all fueling one another's fires when we cultivate the passions we were gifted and graced with. Living in your maximum potential will generate joy from those who love you. You cannot experience trying to conform to a space that doesn't fit you. When you open yourself up to be who only you can be, the impact of fulfillment permeates those around you and inspires them to be more of themselves, and this creates more self-confidence and joy.

Give others the liberty to be themselves and have options. Being the first on a path is not always comfortable. In fact, it is rather scary, and most of the journey is spent with loving onlookers encouraging you to get back to the safe route because they don't want to see you hurt or disappointed. Don't fret over that. We all have to live our own lives and learn our own lessons that produce the character we need.

5. **You will not disappoint people as much as you fear**

Another stronghold for me was fear of disappointing others. I endured situations and circumstances that I knew were unhealthy, unproductive, and ungodly for the sake of trying to make others happy. When we are terrified by the

F. Y. I.

idea of being a disappointment to those whose opinions really matter to us, we can create an emotional prison that stifles our growth.

Consequently, the people who genuinely love you will continue to love you despite the challenges you face. If their love changes, perhaps it wasn't unconditional love in the first place, so don't worry about that. In addition, you do not have to publicize every decision you make. Take time to work through your options and processes, seeking counsel from subject matter experts in the area where you need help. Also, if it is a choice between suffering and safety, your loved ones always want you to choose safety. Finally, everyone has experienced an adverse outcome. Therefore, others will understand when you experience yours. You may even find this to be a good opportunity for those you admire to share their experiences that may be very similar to yours.

Many times when I found the courage to speak with a mentor about a struggle I in my life they shared how they were in a similar place in their lives at one point. This creates an opportunity for your mentor to encourage and build you up, as well as offer tools they used to navigate and overcome problems.

Disappointment is a temporary emotion.
Unconditional love is a permanent state.

THE TOUGHEST MASTER

All of the points listed prior to this are hindrances to freedom based on other people. All of that is actually the easy part to get free from. Some of you may have gotten to

F. Y. I.

this point and said, "I don't fit into any of those categories. I don't have any masters. I'm good LaChish." Then, my response to you would be, to keep reading!

Overcoming the opinions of people is a journey. For those who have reached that point in life, you can attest that it is very liberating! When you can place a barrier around your sanity and heart, and keep everyone else in their rightful, appropriate, and designated place, it grants you clarity and peace that cannot be described. It's like watching the waves of a beautiful blue ocean during sunrise or sunset. It's serene. It's calming. It's a place you always want to escape back to. It's a mental staycation resort.

For many years, my master was other people. Then, I declared my own emancipation proclamation from people and expected to be free forever. Unfortunately, I was not because there was a stronger master I had yet to break free from. That master was me. You may think, "How can I be my own master? How could I be the cause of my own slavery? I thought slavery was when someone else was in control. I thought I was supposed to be the master of my soul LaChish. What are you talking about?"

When someone who has been incarcerated for most of his or her life is released into society, it can be overwhelming and uncomfortable that they would rather go back to prison. To the general population, this seems asinine. Who would want to go back to prison? Who would rather be in prison than out free? However, I have personally witnessed the institutionalized mindset that has made peace with being incarcerated. While the inmate does not enjoy being incarcerated, it has become more familiar than daily living on the outside. Prison is a structured environment where the inmates learn what to expect from day to day. While it can be an extremely dangerous

F. Y. I.

environment, it can also be an escape from the harsh realities of the inadequacies of civilian life.

We can become accustomed to functionally living in dysfunction. Breaking free from what can be the most treacherous task. No one can tear you down further than you. No one can break you down more quickly than you. No one can find fault faster than you. No one can disqualify you better than you. I can testify that no one has stifled my life more than I have. It's always been my internal voice that is my greatest influence. When that voice is toxic, everything in my life becomes infected with poison.

When I began seeking this freedom journey, I thought I needed freedom from everyone else. It was easier to blame others. I legitimately thought it was their fault. Logically, I could justify my case against each defendant in the courtroom of my heart. I was the judge, jury, prosecutor, and bailiff. My perception was my prison. I'd love to pretend that there were only four walls to my prison, but there were so many that it made me think I wasn't in prison at all. I can now share the most prominent hindrances to my personal freedom.

VISION

As I was looking through the *Merriam-Webster Dictionary* for the definition of perception, I came across a powerful paragraph that grouped synonyms together and spoke exactly to the intent of this point. It also reminded me there are multiple layers to the perception I must address to do justice to your freedom journey. "A power to see what is not evident to the average mind" is achieved through discernment, discrimination, perception, penetration, insight, and acumen."[33]

F. Y. I.

A critical discriminator for how an adverse event affects my life is how I view the situation. My vision and understanding of the situation while I'm in it, and especially after I've come through it, determines whether I am better or bitter afterward. If it is not obvious by now, I am a thinker. I think through a situation so many times and from so many different angles that I can wear a situation out. I didn't realize how abnormal this was until I was discussing this with a friend, who I consider another great thinker. My friend was completely finished with the discussion but I was still continuing.

Our vision of life is shaped by many factors. It is shaped by our experiences. It is shaped by our exposure. It is shaped by our education, not just academic but practical life lessons. Several years ago, my vision began changing. I'm speaking of my physical vision. My eyes had been healthy my entire life, although both of my parents wear glasses. All my grandparents wore glasses. Even my great-grandmother wore glasses. I did not need glasses. When I was around 26 or 27 years old, I began noticing words were a little blurry in the distance, but I ignored it. I remember blaming it on my pregnancy, so I just assumed after I had Judah, my vision would return to its original perfect state. However, it did not.

I began noticing I could not see more objects in the distance while others around me would try to have me look at something. I went into a state of denial. I did not want to wear glasses. I already look like my dad's twin, so if I put glasses on, I would turn into him. Glasses were not cute at that time, and I didn't want to look like a "nerd." I was young and more focused on being cute than seeing. I continued a few more years, and every annual eye exam I would cheat. I would look at the eye chart up close before I had to read it from the designated distance. I would either

F. Y. I.

memorize the lowest line, or I would look through my fingers of the eye I was supposed to be covering. I could see better with both eyes than one, therefore, I cheated. I know it sounds pitiful now, but it was that serious for me at the time. It wasn't until I was lying in bed and couldn't see the *TV Guide* that I even acknowledged my vision was a problem. I waited until I literally could not read the words on my 50-inch tv screen to admit I had a vision problem. Then I began noticing when I drove at night that I had a hard time reading the street signs. The GPS would say, turn in 500 meters on X street, but I couldn't see X on the sign, so I would miss my turn and get frustrated.

On my next annual eye exam, I stopped cheating. I told the technician, "*I need to have a thorough eye exam because I'm having trouble reading at a distance.*" I eventually received my first pair of glasses. They were acceptable. I didn't love them. I didn't wear them at all times. I kept them in my car for night use, or when it rained. And I kept a pair on my nightstand and only used them to read the *TV Guide*. I lost them more than wore them. Thus, my vision just kept getting worse. Now, I cannot even see faces clearly in the distance. If I sit in the back of my church or lecture hall without my glasses, I cannot see the presenter's face without looking at the screen, so I wear my glasses every day. I started a year ago when I entered graduate school. If I pull out of my garage without my glasses, I literally turned around to get them because I can tell a huge difference without them. Why am I telling you this?

How clear your vision is determines if you see correctly or not.

F. Y. I.

Without my glasses, I cannot tell the difference between an "F" and a "P". I cannot determine one person from the next by face. My physical vision was not the only vision impaired. My view on life and experiences was also in need of correction. I suspect you could use a vision check as well.

Discernment

Our ability to judge accurately is frequently used in reference to judging someone's character, nature, or intent. The judgment we make here provides the screen or lens through which we evaluate a person's actions. If we discern that people are good, we typically view most of their actions as good, whether they are or not. If we discern that people are deceiving, we typically view everything they say as a lie, whether it is or not. Accuracy or inaccuracy of judgment creates the tone for the story you create about yourself, others, and situations.

The danger in discernment is that prior experience can tint our lens. If we are not careful, we will assume everything that looks alike is the same. If we have been hurt by a certain person, and we meet someone who reminds us of the old person it's extremely difficult for the new person. We are no longer discerning. All accuracy is lost. We must always be careful to wear our corrective lenses since the details and the ability to differentiate matter.

Discrimination

How well can you recognize the difference between two or more situations? We often see discrimination in the negative connotation of unjust treatment based on characteristics or traits. However, in the context of your life

F. Y. I.

visual acuity, discrimination is a positive and essential component.

We can view life experiences as either attacks against us or opportunities for us to grow.

We can view people as our haters or as tools to sharpen us. We can view ourselves as victims barely trying to survive or as more than conquerors determined to overcome every challenge we face. We can view our circumstances as hopeful or hopeless. The choice we make in discrimination continues the script for the story we are telling ourselves. The problem is that if we make the wrong determination our stories are fictitious, but we are using them for non-fictional application.

Perception

Next, there is a perception which involves your senses. Physical perception is exercised in every moment. You're doing it right now and not even thinking about it. It's the sum of what you're seeing, hearing, feeling, smelling, and possibly tasting that puts you at ease or on alert. Deeper than your physical senses, I want you to awaken and sharpen your mental, emotional, and spiritual senses. This determines the way you interpret and make sense of life.

Believe it or not, every day in every situation you are developing a story. You are developing a way to rationalize and remember the events of your life. You recall the major events most easily because they have the most elaborate stories. The menial experiences get a bland,

F. Y. I.

boring story that you tend to forget. Your perception determines your story category. You perceive it as a drama, romance, thriller, horror, comedy, suspense, etc. You will fill in the gaps. You will sometimes exaggerate the facts with what aids you in the ultimate finale you need to justify your storyline. If you need to be the victim, you will make someone the villain. If you need to be the victor, you will make someone the adversary. If you need to be right, you will make someone wrong. If you need to be special, you will make others inferior.

You winning should not come at the expense of someone else losing.

This creative storytelling process is going to happen. Framing life through a positive lens affords hope, strength, control, and liberty to produce the stories where you always win. However, if you frame your life or experiences through a saga of setbacks, you voluntarily enter a prison of victimhood. You are the director. You get to interpret how the audience will view the content of your life.

Penetration

Throughout the course of each day, there are multiple exchanges and interactions. They do not all impact us the same way, and often, we never even give conscious thought to some interactions. Think about when you walk in a public place. You can pass by several people and never see their faces or recall them afterward. You walk past several stores, looking for the one you're interested in at the mall. I've noticed that I can receive the same comment from multiple people, but it affects me differently

F. Y. I.

depending on my relationship with the person speaking it. Likewise, how I perceive a situation determines how deeply it penetrates me.

I have experienced various trials and tribulations over the course of my life. The deepest wounds have all been connected to perceiving that someone maliciously intended to harm me. When someone that I trusted behaved in a way that caused hurt, I automatically assumed they did it to hurt me. Nowhere in my discernment, discrimination, or perception was I able to see higher, broader, or deeper into the true story they were telling themselves. Their story never mattered while I was constructing mine. This way of thinking and being causes deep rifts, valleys, and seeds of depression in my life. For years, the bottom of my heart was penetrated with layers of stories accounting for and justifying the autobiographic movie I was writing, directing, producing, and replaying as often as I wanted to.

For the longest time, I could not understand why I had to experience painful events. I could not understand why people would want to hurt me. You see, when we are writing our stories, we are always the main character. Everyone else is an extra or supporting cast member. The storyline is about us, how we feel, how it affects us, how we are treated, and how everyone handles us. The problem with this line of thinking is it inevitably depicts us as a victim in uncomfortable exchanges. We are always subject to the choices and decisions of others. Our story is controlled by how others act, instead of how we think, speak, and behave. We are always at the mercy of another person. We have become a passenger, riding in everyone else's vehicle, instead of driving our own lives.

When I really asked GOD to clarify my vision, my life's story took a drastic turn from victimization to compassion and victory. I looked back on the people whose

F. Y. I.

actions hurt me and saw that they rarely hurt me intentionally. They were hurting themselves. Sometimes, I was part of collateral damage. Certainly, I thought I should have been important enough to factor into the equation for their decision-making process. I thought I was important enough to deter and alter their choices.

I understand now our mindsets are comprised of extremely complex circuits. Oxymorons exist.

It is possible for someone to love you and unintentionally hurt you. It is possible for someone to want to treat you as you deserve, but because he/she is wrestling with his/her own mental anguish, he/she cannot experience transformation. It is possible for good people to have bad character traits. It is possible for people to excel in one area of their lives and be completely stunted in another area of their lives.

I have learned, and am learning more than ever that everyone is living in their own movie. We only allow others to see the parts of our movie we are proud of. We replay the parts that elicit the most positive light and reflect the person we want to be entirely even if we have not quite attained that.

The moment I accepted my responsibility to accurately assess, analyze, and affirm the difficult situations I faced was the moment I became free.

When I took responsibility for the accessibility of my heart in trying times, life changed. I was no longer a victim, subject to whatever happened. Instead, I was able to

F. Y. I.

see others through the lens of compassion, grace, and empathy. In doing this, my heart began uprooting all the negative storylines, and the chains were swept out. I choose daily to safeguard my heart.

It is my aim to deny toxicity access to penetrate my mind, heart, or spirit.

Insight

The moment I invited GOD into my production team was the moment insight became a part of my daily existence. Insight is a deeper perspective and understanding. I like to think about the eagle's view. The eagle soars so high but has a keen vision.

Eagle view is my goal view. It is high enough to assess the entire scene, but keen enough to focus on its target.

I love to fly for two reasons. One, I can get to my destination faster than driving. Second, I can view the earth from a higher perspective. When I stand on the ground, everything is bigger than I am. The houses and buildings are big. The vehicles are big. In congested or metropolitan areas, there are many structures that make it difficult to see in the distance. When I fly, I watch as we take off and how much smaller everything gets when we go up.

Sometimes, you have to take a break and go UP! Up in your thinking. Up in your praying. Up in your reading.

F. Y. I.

Up in your focus. Up in your forgiveness. Up in your compassion. Up in your love. Up in your kindness. Up in your grace. Up in your patience. Up in your sensitivity. Up in your existence. You don't have to stay in low places. Spread your wings and mount up like eagles. Take flight! It's your choice.

When I was a teenager Tracie, my mentor at that time who has become my best friend, used to tell me frequently "Don't sweat the small stuff." As a teenager, nothing is small! Everything is a major deal! I can laugh at my children now, especially my teenagers. The concerns that are insignificant to me as an adult can be very significant to them. I'm not worried about the tags on my clothes. I'm more concerned with the balance in my savings account. I don't care if I have the newest pair of shoes. I'm more concerned with whether my children can still fit in the shoes I just bought their two months ago. I am not worried about impressing people watching me. I am more concerned with being steadfast in my commitments.

Your insight is growing my friend. The fact that you're reading this book, and other books, tells me that you are working to elevate your view of life. You are on an upward journey, and what used to seem MAJOR will become small. You will stop looking for people to offend you. Instead, take that extra step when someone is behaving in a manner that is unpleasant in order to explore what is happening in that individual's life. We have to avoid being egocentric, thinking everything is only about us and not considering the heart of others. I do understand. Some people appear to be mean for no reason at all. I promise you; there is a reason. When babies are born, they have a personality, but generally, they are going through the same developmental stages as every other baby their age. Their environment and experiences shape their

F. Y. I.

personalities over time, along with some genetic components. I have experienced this frequently with adults behaving in a dysfunctional manner. When people experience trauma to their psyche or mind, their natural age continues to advance with time, but they are literally trapped in the day that trauma occurred until they can successfully process it and fix the storyline. Their age may be forty, but their mind is still eight.

Whenever you reach a difficult narrative in your story, stop and think higher!

Acumen

We have explored discernment, discrimination, perception, penetration, insight, and now let's look at acumen. Acumen is so important because this is your ability to make good judgments quickly. Of course, there will be life events that you have time to prepare for and scrutinize for hours and days, even before making a decision. However, there are many times when you must make a judgment call spontaneously, and this is where you will learn to succeed or fail. Your instinctive reaction must change from the default negative frame society has labeled as realism. We have to retrain our thinking so that our first response is favorable to our freedom journey and lifestyle.

I cannot count how many times I have lost control during a tense situation and spoke words that I would not have said if I had time to think about them first. Now, this is unusual to say because one of the most common descriptions people use for me is a calm demeanor, not frazzled or ruffled easily or at all. I had an instructor evaluate me in the clinic, and she said, "LaChish, I love how you have a serene tone and demeanor during your patient encounters. If I were your patient, I would feel comfortable telling you anything." In addition, when I get

F. Y. I.

up for public speaking opportunities, I have received compliments for how comfortable I am on stage. What these outward observations fail to reveal is in my mind there are multiple conversations going on to calm my nerves, to silence my anxiety, and to prevent my adverse reactions from coming across in my demeanor.

However, I am a young woman who was born and raised in Philadelphia. Philadelphia is a city where children learn very young how to become aggressive, defensive, and have a low tolerance for feeling insulted. Unfortunately, I have witness people injured or murdered for actions other places I have lived would deem trivial. There are so many great characteristics I gained from living in that city, but interpersonal conflict resolution was not perfected there. I am a South Philly girl who moved to North Philly for my teenage years. My family is very emotional and vocal. We are also known for throwing up our hands without a second thought. I have to talk South Philly Chish off of many ledges, hold her back, shut her up, and sit her down. When I face situations that really penetrate and pluck a nerve, I am tempted to be Ce-Ce. Ce-Ce is the nickname my family calls me. Most of them don't call me by my name even today. For me, Ce-Ce is a quiet storm. Ce-Ce can go from a quiet, meek, humble girl to the Incredible Hulk.

My calm demeanor is the norm for me. I think my brother Iric, my dad, and I have very similar personalities. We are all fairly calm. My dad, Mr. Pete, and I are probably more reserved and introverted until we are around people whose company we really enjoy. My dad is certainly more outgoing than I am in that he will talk to strangers everywhere without a problem. However, my mother, Marsheila, is an absolute extrovert. She doesn't go ANYWHERE without making a friend. She strikes up a conversation with someone everywhere she goes. I admire

F. Y. I.

that about her. She is not shy unless she's around conceited church people. Otherwise, she will tell you her life story and mine. She will break into a dance whenever she hears music. She was the "cool" mom when I was a child to all of my friends, but the embarrassing mom for me because I was more shy and reserved. One commonality my parents, brother, and I share is that we can breathe the fire of anger when we face a situation that annoys us the most! We can go THERE! We all have baby dragons that breathe fire when we allow them to. My mom's dragon probably breathes the most frequent, but she's calmed down so much as her experience of life has changed. My father's dragon breathes when he's receiving poor customer service, or someone has mishandled his money or family. Iric's dragon breathes when he has been pushed to his limits, and people are always shocked when it happens. My dragon used to breathe whenever someone called me a female dog. The "B" word will never be an acceptable title for me. If someone hurts my children, the fire of my anger can consume, and honestly, my spouse has been the only one to get burned up in the most recent years. My sisters- Davida, Faith, and Michelle- breathe their fire when someone tries to hurt anyone of us. My oldest brother, Larry, is our true Beast Mode bro. He is kind UNTIL the family is threatened in any way. Last my stepmother, Mrs. Debbie, tries to only breathe her fire in prayer.

    I learned very early in my military career that South Philly Chish would hinder my progress. I sharpened my acumen publicly. I also had to sharpen my acumen privately. I had to make quick judgment calls on how I would engage or diffuse a situation. The most effective way I began changing my instinctive reaction was tracing my trigger points and guarding them with my life. It's like a thermostat in a public building that is kept in a box and requires a key to access the thermostat. Even some fire

F. Y. I.

alarms are placed higher as well as extinguishers and axes behind glass. The glass or plastic is there to prevent accidental alarms or to keep inappropriate people from accessing the equipment. The thermostat and fire alarm affect the entire population within the building.

Now I have just given you three known triggers for me, so how do I properly respond in the heat of the moment? First, I consider the person attempting to turn the heat up on my thermostat. Is this a person who adds value to my life? Yes or no? If not, they don't deserve access to my thermostat. They don't get the key. My temperature will remain calm and serene. If this person normally adds value to my life, what is the real issue right now? Is the individual hurt and disappointed in something I said, did, or neglected to say or do? If so, was I aware of this offense I caused? Can I apologize now and diffuse the situation? Is the offense accurate? Sometimes people can think your comments, thoughts, or behaviors are directed towards them when they are not. Misunderstandings can easily be resolved when clarity is brought. I minimize the negative energy in my life and do not allow others to surpass my personal limit. In other words, will this issue matter five hours, days, weeks, months, or years from now if it is not engaged? If the answer is no, I ignore it!

Without a vision, you will perish! You have to establish a clear vision for your life. Who are you? Why are you here on earth? What is your purpose? What are your gifts? What can you contribute to the world? Where is your goal destination? What type of movie is your life?

When I established Simply LaChish business, I was asked what my brand would mean and stand for. It is an extension of my personal vision for my life. I walk and live by faith, in a thriller where the good guys win in the end! However, there are whimsical moments. There's certainly comedy and philosophical themes. There's love threaded throughout my life. There will certainly be a little drama, mystery, and conflict. I enjoy the magical realism. My point is that regardless of the twists and turns by the end of my journey on earth, I want my movie to be inspirational to everyone who encounters me.

I think about two of my favorite actors, Will Smith and Denzel Washington. I know in every movie with Will Smith, I'm going to laugh, feel good, and maybe cry. Whenever I watch a Denzel Washington movie, it's guaranteed I'm going to cry at some point. I'm going to get fully sucked in and experience the emotional rollercoasters of the cast involved. They have their known strengths, and we've grown to love them for it. What do people expect from your movie? What are you known for? What do you want to be known for? Clarify your vision and make sure your storyline consistently relays that message. When a writer begins a story, everything included must point to and build upon the ultimate goal. As you live from day to day, keep your ultimate goals in mind.

EVICTION NOTICE

Take a moment to evict every internal hindrance you've plagued yourself with:

1. Shame
2. Unforgiveness of self
3. Lack of trust in self
4. Pride
5. Ignorance
6. Low-self esteem
7. Feeling undeserving of good things
8. Loneliness

F. Y. I.

9. Guilt
10. Self-hate
11. Self-sabotage
12. Fill in your own characteristics/actions _____

There are some mental strongholds that you have battled far too long, and you don't feel capable of freeing yourself from. Know there are people strategically placed around you who can help you break free. I will never forget Pastor Valencia Hines in Columbus Georgia, taking time one evening to pray with me. I was in my early twenties, and I was wrestling with my identity. I was wrestling with my spiritual identity. I was wrestling with my natural identity. I was wrestling with my sexual identity. I was wrestling with my emotional identity. I felt conflicted gravely. What I felt and what I knew were not lining up. While I was a light to so many other young people, I was sinking privately. I could never understand how people lived contradictory public and private lives, and I didn't want to be that person. I remember walking in her church one evening while she was in her office, handling some administrative tasks. I didn't even have to tell her what was wrong. I just looked at her and said, "I can't live like this." She stopped what she was doing and began to pray for me. She took the authority I was not equipped to take. She had the courage I did not have. She had the faith I did not have. She interceded for me. She did for me what I could not do for myself. She helped get me to the other side of the storm.

There are times when you have to lay down your pride, image, and desire to "protect" yourself and allow someone who is capable of helping you step in. Find that person you can be honest with. Find someone who doesn't require all the details to offer their help. Find someone who can keep you accountable. Find someone who can correct you when

F. Y. I.

you're wrong. Find someone who loves you more than you love yourself. Find someone who has more faith than you. Find someone who has more wisdom than you. Find someone who has more strength than you in that area. Find someone who doesn't mind fighting for your victory as they would fight for their own. I promise there is more than one person in your reach that is willing to help you. Take a moment to look around you.

The beauty in this journey is once you have done everything you're responsible for, and others have done all they can do for you without full relief. You can go to the FATHER and ask HIM to free you from the chains you cannot break. Even if you have not been a person of faith in the past or are skeptical of the presence of GOD, there is no risk in trying. It is not a difficult process. All it requires is a sincere heart.

I have cried to GOD for deliverance and freedom at many junctions. The times when I walked away successfully were the times when I openly shared my heart with HIM. The blessing in prayer is you don't have to format it in a special way. You simply talk to GOD for yourself. I have spent time talking, sometimes crying, sometimes just worshipping, sometimes a combination of it all. I will let you into my prayer closet, which is something I don't normally do. I want you to feel completely confident in getting your own freedom. The power is not in the words you or I choose to use, but in the sincerity of our hearts when we seek the FATHER. HE wants better for you than you want for yourself. Trust me!

The simplest way is to say, "FATHER, HELP ME!"

But if you need to say more, then you can begin with this and flow from there:

F. Y. I.

FATHER, I am troubled. I have fears. I have doubts. I have anger and even hatred built up. I have embarrassing habits and addictions. I have thoughts I'm ashamed to admit. You know everything about me already. I do not understand YOUR ways or methods. But I am trying to experience freedom. I don't even feel as if I deserve it, but I want it. I need it. I need YOU to help me let go. I have tried my best to make my life work. I have tried my best to be a good person. I have even tried to be a bad person to those who hurt me. I have tried my best to live. I am struggling. There are some situations I have together, and I thank YOU for them. But these strongholds in my mind, body, soul, and spirit, I just cannot overcome by myself. I am trusting YOU to guide me through the process of being made whole. I didn't even realize how broken I was until now. I didn't know how hurt I was until now. I didn't realize how desperate I was until now.

Please, set my mind free from the memories that torment me. Please, set my heart free from the emotions that weigh me down. Please, set my spirit free from the chains that keep me from YOUR presence. I want to be free. I want to be whole. I want to be pure. I want to be strong. I want to be happy. I want to be joyful. I want to be at peace. I want to feel secure. I want to feel YOUR love. I want to be what YOU created me to be. Help me to love myself. Help me to forgive myself. Help me to give myself permission to be happy and to be blessed. Set me free from myself. I thank YOU for making me free and equipping me with the discipline to stay free from this moment forward. AMEN

F. Y. I.

Chapter Nine

Do the Root Work

How long have you been a fruit inspector? We analyze and judge from the behavior or final product. We inspect the fruit. If it's sweet to our taste, we are good with it. If it tastes less than optimal, we can become skeptical. In the last chapter, we spent some time dealing with some fruit, some branches, and maybe some trunks. We took a moment to pray for liberty. I believe that liberty has been made available. The ability to maintain that liberty lies within your willingness to uproot the roots and guard your soil. In order for us to win, we have to get down into the dirt and expose the roots.

Exposing the roots is often the first step in fixing the produce, but we also must inspect the seeds being sown. What if I told you every disappointment, struggle, stronghold, habit, addiction, and any kind of suffering began with the same seed? We tend to view situations from the outside in, instead of the inside out. We judge what we can observe and forget there are roots leading to that fruit. If you focus on changing the fruit and never work on changing the seed, the water, the nutrients, or the light you have provided to produce the fruit, you will have only temporary success. At this point in your life, changing is not enough. You need a complete transformation.

F. Y. I.

Transformation can only take place from the dirt. But where is the dirt? Or maybe the soil would be a better term.

In a garden, I think of seeds, soil, and fruit. In the course of a day, I think of events, thoughts, reactions, and results. Many times, instead of responding to an event, we have a reflex reaction. Reflexes are responses produced with minimal cognitive effort. Physical reflexes are involuntary neurological responses, but your emotional and mental reflexes are short-cuts you have developed through experiences. Some physical reflexes you may relate to occur when your healthcare provider taps your knee with a tool, and your leg kicks out. When you hear a loud noise, and your head turns in the direction of the noise, that is a reflex. When you sneeze, your eyes closing is an automatic reflex. These are all experiences that happen without deliberate effort. Emotional reflexes I have encountered and/or observed work the same way.

Also, offense has become a reflex. When you speak to someone who does not speak back, it could cause offense. If you're driving, and someone cuts you off, it could cause offense. If someone pursues a romantic encounter with someone you're already romantically involved with could cause offense. If someone on your team at work is acknowledged or promoted, but you have been working harder, it could cause offense. If you have an important life event, and someone you really expected to attend doesn't show up, it could cause offense. Offenses can occur in several situations and settings. They can present as a small shift in your body language, angry words, physical expressions of disgust, an irate attitude, or an ongoing side conversation about the person after every encounter. The size of the offense is not the focus here. Rather, it is the fact being offended has become so easy in

𝓕. 𝒴. 𝐼.

today's society. It has become a natural reflex for many. It was not always this way, so where does it come from?

I wanted to provide principles that could be applied to any person, at any junction or situation. The only way this would work is if every outcome had the same beginning. Rest assured, it does. If you recall, I mentioned in a prior chapter that we are all creating a story of our life. This story is not one we frequently verbalize. In fact, you are often writing without thinking about it. You know how it is to be driving or going to a familiar place, on a familiar route, in a familiar climate, and you travel absent-mindedly. There are many days I have driven to work with my mind preoccupied and couldn't tell you how I got from my driveway to the parking lot. I wasn't texting on my phone or driving physically distracted, but my mind was busy while my body repeated the same actions it did many times before when I was deliberately paying attention. In this case, it's a very good natural response. Sometimes repetition is not always as beneficial.

I wish I could tell you some new revelation that has never been expressed before. I wish I could take credit for a ground-breaking philosophy. Actually, there is nothing new under the sun. Everything that is, was and is to be, began with the same seed. That seed is a word. Before we can get to the words that come out of your mouth, we must start at the beginning with the words breeding in your mind, your thoughts.

In every moment, your mind is speaking to you. It is constantly responding to both internal and external triggers. Every experience produces an initial thought that creates the tone for how the total experience will be framed, felt, and filed. Remember this sequence:

F. Y. I.

ROOT-TO-FRUIT

Once your senses are engaged in an activating event you discover the following:

1. You have a **thought**—This thought is simple and driven by instinct. You accept or reject it. Once you accept
2. Then, you produce a **feeling**— a response to the keywords in the initial thought
3. You produce an **emotion**—possessing the initial feeling but more powerful. The emotion makes an impression on you. The stronger the emotion, the stronger the impression.
4. You produce an **action**— an outward expression of the internal process that has begun. This is the first time others are exposed to the seed. The action could be the terminal end, or it can continue to progress depending on how gratifying the response to your action was.
5. You produce a **behavior**—this is the way you conduct yourself. The action could be as simple as a facial expression, gesture, or isolated act. The action is similar to the preview trailer or commercial. The behavior becomes the actual show or movie.
6. You incur a **habit**—Behaviors that produce gratification are easily turned into habits. Behaviors become habits with repetition over the course of weeks. Habits are easier to continue than break.
7. You create your **character**—Your character is the sum of all your habits. Whether your character is notable or flawed has everything to do with how

F. Y. I.

you manage your habits or mismanage them. Your character is how your reputation is established.

8. Your **struggles** surface when a flawed character is left unchecked
9. You form **strongholds** when pride prevents you from seeking help with your struggles
10. Your **lifestyle** becomes the fruit of your most prevalent thoughts.

That is a quick breakdown of the sequential products of a single thought. There is so much more occurring in between the steps. At every step, you have a crossroad of whether you will continue on the path or terminate it. The choice to continue is commonly based on the emotional deficit you are trying to fulfill. The emotional deficit is determined by the storyline you have purposed in your heart to manifest. It's not enough for me to expose the process if I don't equip you with how to take control of your own life.

I learned this in my own life. In a class I took, the students were instructed to develop a root cause analysis of a workplace problem we wanted to resolve. At the time, I identified a safety concern with the medical technicians turning away patients that were a high risk during sick-call hours. The rule of the clinic was for patients to check-in between 0600-0700 for an acute medical condition acquired within the last 72 hours. If patients checked in for an issue that was ongoing for greater than 72 hours, a scheduled appointment should be made. Sick-call clinic appointments were supposed to last 5-15 minutes, designed to stabilize an issue to prevent worsening conditions and a follow up as needed. The rule was clear. The problem came when patients with red flag complaints were turned away

F. Y. I.

because they checked in either after 0700 or stated the initial symptoms began 72 hours or greater. One key example which brought this problem to light was a patient with abdominal pain and fever. The patient was turned away although the patient was presenting with appendicitis. This condition typically results in immediate surgical intervention.

On the surface, it would appear the medical technicians were the problem here. It was obviously the front desk screener who asked the questions, resulting in the patient being sent away. On further assessment, I met with the team of medical technicians to get their perspective. They were following the standard protocol. Many of the medics were new to the military and even newer to the medical field. Their training had primarily in combat and trauma. Clinical signs of medical conditions were not their strength. They were blanketly following the rule. No one had taken the time to train them on exceptions to the rule.

Who was responsible for the medical technicians' proficiency? Several people were responsible. Their medical provider was charged with training their unit medics to standard. The person whom the technician followed during orientation, their preceptor, was responsible for the practical application of the standard operating procedures. The senior medic in their company, battalion, and brigade was responsible for continued education and maintaining their skill proficiency. As the brigade nurse, I had a role to play to help sharpen their clinical judgment. By the time the root analysis was complete, we realized the problem was a lack of education. The staff was not equipped with the fundamental tools in the clinical setting. It was resolved with a series of classes I created, teaching the brigade medics how to properly triage patients in a clinical setting. They learned how to screen the

F. Y. I.

patients and what pertinent questions to ask while preparing a report for their medical provider. The problem was solved, at least for that group of medics. It would be their job, as well as their leadership's responsibility, to ensure all staff members received the pertinent information to prevent unnecessary medical complications.

If I stopped at the surface of the perceived problem, I would have disciplined a few medics for their bad choice. Those few employees may not have made a mistake again, but it wasn't an individual problem. It was a systemic problem. I was conducting the same process with my personal life. I was tackling problems from what they looked like on the surface. There were times when I would "fix" it. I would cut it off. I didn't realize the reason the issues continued to come back was that I never addressed the root.

What major concerns in your life have you failed to complete a root cause analysis on? Let's trace a few popular ones.

1. HEALTH

Your physical health is a combination of your genetics and your decisions: actions, behaviors, habits, struggles…lifestyle. If you're overweight, the first look is nutrition and exercise. How many calories are you taking in versus how many are you burning each day? If you don't exercise, your medical provider will share all of the benefits of 30 minutes of cardiovascular activity 3-5 days a week. Surely it is beneficial for your heart health, blood pressure, cholesterol, glucose, weight, and even your mental health. What are you eating? How much of it? How

F. Y. I.

often? It's got to be the food! Right? What if the root of the problem has nothing to do with food?

Food is necessary for our physical sustainment and development. Overindulging can be seen as a habit or addiction. What I know to be a cause of overeating is using food for comfort? When we are celebrating something, we eat. When we are upset over something, we eat. Depression can cause overeating. Insecurity can cause overeating. Overcompensating can cause overeating. Even here, we're dealing with feelings and emotions. What is the root? What are you telling yourself about your current health?

Root: I am scared of being rejected. I have found a way to keep people away from me to prevent getting hurt.

Root: I don't want to lose myself. I've always been this way. Changing now would be selling out on myself. This is who I am. My identity is wrapped in my physical appearance. I don't know who I would be if I changed.

Root: I went to bed hungry too many times when I was a child. I promised myself I would never go hungry again. I watched my mom go without so she could feed me. It used to be a privilege to eat. Now, it's my passion.

Root: I love to cook. I'm good at cooking. I cook too much, and I don't want to waste food. I was taught never to waste food. Food is how I get people to come around me. Food represents fellowship and love for me.

Root: It doesn't matter how much I do or do not eat, my weight doesn't change. I'm sick of hearing about it. Everyone isn't meant to be skinny.

Point: It's not about the food. It's about the thoughts surrounding body image and food.

F. Y. I.

The same goes for smoking, excessive drinking, high-risk behaviors, non-compliance with taking prescribed medications, etc. It's not about the cigarettes, cigar, marijuana, drugs, alcohol, sexual promiscuity, jumping out of planes, riding motorcycles without helmets or vehicles at extreme speeds. Those are all fruits of a thought.

2. RELATIONSHIPS

If you have a relationship that you're not content with, platonic or romantic, what is the true root? I spent years looking at what other people were or weren't doing for me. I needed people to feel complete. I hated being by myself. I still don't like eating out in a restaurant by myself. I have never been to the movies by myself. I can stay home all day, week, month by myself, but going out in public, I just became uncomfortable. I started wearing earphones to listen to music, or I would have to talk to someone on the phone while I was out so I could have "company." I reached a place where I didn't realize how much I was depending on external affirmation to be happy. I was always crushed when someone disappointed me, insulted me, or rejected me. I gave people multiple chances after blatantly hurting and disregarding my emotional well-being because I was desperate for the validation I felt from having their friendship or companionship.

Disappointment was inevitable for me because I thought the problem was people taking advantage of my kindness. The problem was never the other person. The root cause of every imbalance I was experiencing was due to the storyline I was subconsciously feeding myself. It's possible your relationships are suffering from the same problem: your thoughts about YOU!

F. Y. I.

Root: I've never been the cutest girl in the group. I am not physically attractive enough to demand commitment.

Root: I don't love all of me. I have to make sure I shower people with what I can. That way they will love me. Just being me isn't enough to elicit love.

Root: I've been betrayed, and I cannot emotionally handle that. I keep everyone at a distance. Everyone must be disposable. I cannot invest too much in people because anyone can hurt me at any second. I have to let them know I don't need anyone.

Root: Maybe, the reason why I can't keep a relationship is because I'm not good enough. Even giving my best efforts, does not always work out for me.

Root: I must have done something to deserve this treatment. I'll pay my debt.

Root: I'm no one without them.

Point: People will treat you the way you let them treat you. It doesn't take long for people to sense how you feel about yourself, and if you're not careful, they will leverage the opportunity. Love yourself first, and you'll be surprised how many people love you just for who you are. You'd be surprised how amazing you are to others you've never given an opportunity to share.

There is nothing that anyone can provide for you if you do not feel worthy to receive it. You will ruin it every time to prove you were right about not deserving it.

F. Y. I.

3. CAREER

Have you hit the ceiling in the career path you've chosen? Or have you lost fulfillment from the job? Are you working just to pay bills? Or do you love what you do? Traditionally, we are spending 40 hours a week working. A majority of our life is spent at work and asleep. If your workplace is unfulfilling or miserable, consider the number of negative thoughts you produce and entertain on a daily basis. What is keeping you from going into the career field you actually want to be in? Is your current job the problem? Is the paycheck the problem?

What is the root? Have you applied yourself 100%? Are you investing your gifts, time, and efforts into the success of the mission? Are you passionate about the purpose of the company? Is your motive the check or the impact? These factors matter when it comes to your acceleration. Even for those who have done everything they know how to make it work, what are you telling yourself while you wait to reap your harvest?

Root: I'm not smart enough to get the prerequisites for the career I really want. I know my place.

Root: I don't have anyone to help me make it happen.

Root: I need the check more than I need the fulfillment. Fulfillment isn't paying my bills each month.

Root: I'm doing better than many people. Shouldn't I be grateful for that?

Root: I don't want to leave my friends and family behind. Going after what I want means, I have to step out of my current circle.

Root: This is the hand I've been dealt. Better doesn't happen to people like me.

F. Y. I.

Point: Every one of us has a passion, natural gifts, and abilities that are effortless. The distance between your dream career and your current career is your ability to persevere through the necessary process. YOU are your biggest asset. YOU are your biggest cheerleader. YOU are your biggest promoter. YOU are your biggest help or hindrance. YOU are responsible for bringing your vision to pass. How you see a situation impacts your root, and how you process the situation determines the impact on your life.

YOUR PROCESSOR

What type of processor do you have? Computers, tablets, phones, gaming systems, etc. have technology that allows it to operate. It determines the quality, speed, capacity, capability, etc. I am not a technology buff, so before I use the wrong terminology, let me get to my point. Your mind is your processing center. It is responsible for the quality of your life. It manages the capacity of your potential. It feeds the rate to which you accomplish each goal. It is the springboard for your capability. Your mind is arguably your most valuable asset, so what kind of processor do you have?

When you experience life, how are you processing it? Let's work through a few processing mistakes I have identified.

Activating Event 1: A person does not respond to your communication efforts (text, phone call, message, or email) in the timeframe you expected.

Thought A: They are ignoring me.

F. Y. I.

Thought B: They must be busy.

Thought C: I hope everything is ok with them.

Storyline A: This person is being disrespectful to me, abandoning me when I needed help, and trying to hurt me.

Storyline B: This person has other priorities and will get back with me when he or she can offer a quality response.

Storyline C: Perhaps, I should make sure this person is doing well because this is not like him or her.

Feeling/Emotion A: Annoyed, insulted, angry, pissed, disgruntled, disappointed

Feeling/Emotion B: At peace, patient, secure

Feeling/Emotion C: Concern, respect, empathy

Action A: Call/text/message back and leave a heated message. End the connection. Tell everyone how he or she did you wrong.

Action B: Patiently, wait for a response. In the meantime, work on other things, you have to do. Be productive while you wait. Follow up to make sure the person received your initial contact effort.

Action C: Reach out and ask if everything is all right? Show genuine concern for their well-being.

It's all the same activating event but leads to different actions based on the words you tell yourself about it.

Activating Event 2: A person makes a statement to or about you that you don't like.

Thought A: Bi*$%. They just tried to embarrass me.

F. Y. I.

Thought B: What did they mean?

Thought C: I am not responsible or driven by what others think of or say about me.

Storyline A: Haters are gonna hate. It's time for me to put people in their place.

Storyline B: The misunderstanding deserves additional communication. Let me investigate, clarify, or verify that.

Storyline C: No story is required. Forget about it.

Feeling/Emotion A: Infuriated, anxious, aggressive, confrontational, feeling some type of way, violent

Feeling/Emotion B: Confused, optimistic, curious, hopeful

Feeling/Emotion C: Peace

Action A: Speak up! Put them in their place.

Action B: Ask them to explain what they meant by the statement. Inform them how you took it. Find common ground or agree to disagree.

Action C: Move on with your day.

    The more I grow in life, the less I require from others. I understand that no one owes me anything. They don't owe me respect. They don't owe me love. They don't owe me honor. I owe myself respect. I owe myself love. I owe myself honor. I have to respect my identity independently of the opinions of people. I have to love myself even when others find reasons not to. I have to honor myself and my blood pressure by not allowing every negative comment to make me angry.

    There are many events we can choose from. What I want you to draw from this is the ability to monitor the first thought you have in response to the activating event. Your

F. Y. I.

processor has to be clear and whole. Your mind cannot contain a constant negative newsfeed and produce a productive life.

Let's look at a few serious activating events.

Activating Event 3: Someone violated you physically, sexually, or otherwise.

Thought A: I deserved it.

Thought B: I am ashamed of it.

Thought C: Something is wrong with them.

Storyline A: Everyone who is violated asked for it in some way. I brought this on myself.

Storyline B: I am damaged goods because of this. I have to hide it.

Storyline C: I need to forgive them before I become the very person I hate.

Feeling/Emotion A: Angry with self, self-hate, anxious, hypervigilant, obsessive, hurt

Feeling/Emotion B: Insecure, disgusted, rejected, abandoned, dirty, guilty, hurt

Feeling/Emotion C: Empathetic, secured, confident, compassionate, hurt

Action A: Become promiscuous, use sex as a means of control, use aggression as a sense of control, bash other victims

Action B: Hide it. Keep it a secret. Overcompensate to prove your self-worth or lack thereof. Allow people to use or take advantage of you.

F. Y. I.

Action C: Expose the truth in love. Let justice and GOD vindicate you. Forgive your offender. Use your experience as a tool to empower others; there is life after trauma. Seek the counseling you need to heal from it.

This situation is sensitive and prevalent because many are too afraid to tell. Children are repeatedly violated by the same offenders often because they are paralyzed with fear, anxiety, shame, and thoughts that no one will believe them. Let's stop the cycle. Remove the taboo and open the discussion.

Activating Event 4: A parent chooses not to be a part of your life

Thought A: They don't love me.

Thought B: I ran them off.

Thought C: They weren't equipped to be there.

Storyline A: If my own parents didn't love me, no one else will.

Storyline B: Something is wrong with me, and I should expect everyone to abandon me. No one is trustworthy.

Storyline C: I'm not the first child to grow up with an absent parent. I can make of this what I will.

Feeling/Emotion A: worthless, undeserving of love, less than, powerless, crushed, devastated, desperation, hurt

Feeling/Emotion B: broken, inadequate, dysfunctional, guarded, introverted, hypervigilant, hurt

Feeling/Emotion C: empathetic, hopeful, empowered to control the trajectory of your life, inspired to be better for your future children, invested in your future

F. Y. I.

Action A: Settle for mediocrity. Search for love in all the wrong places. Lower your standards for yourself and others. Expect the worst of everyone.

Action B: Intentionally run people off before they can leave. Sabotage every relationship or opportunity. Take your anger out on the world. Repeat the cycle and abandon your responsibilities.

Action C: Acknowledge your disappointment. Appreciate the surrogate parents in your life. Leverage the teachers, coaches, mentors, friends, and family members who are there for you. Be to someone else what you wish you had. Forgive that parent and love him or her in his/her absence, or presence when he/she returns.

The bottom line with all of these scenarios is:

It is NOT your job to determine the motive for the other person's action. Your freedom is not dependent upon their motive, but your processor!

We can get pretty wrapped up trying to figure out the "why" behind other people's actions, or lack thereof. That is a thinking trap that doesn't serve you well. It is unnecessary to determine other people's motives when you are focused on your response. The reasons why others make the choices they make are as complex as the reasons you make the choices you make. Unless other people clearly offer their reasons for their behavior, it is not an essential piece of your freedom process. Deal with the facts of the situation and less of your opinions. It will serve you better in how you process difficult times. It frees your heart from internalizing motives that belong to other people.

F. Y. I.

Always remember, your complexities and unique characteristics are more than enough for you to figure out.

If you spend your time and energy on the things you can control, you will never waste time on the things you cannot.

YOUR CHOICE

I started paying attention to my mood and I noticed that whatever mood I was in, directly reflected thoughts I was rehearsing in my mind. Every time I found myself in a bad mood, I began taking inventory of my thoughts and replacing them with thoughts more conducive to improving my mood. I want to encourage you to make a conscious effort to pay attention to your thoughts. Those words rolling around in your head are framing your life. If you want to find true freedom, you have to clean up your processor!

The choice of freedom or bondage is in the word you speak in your mind.

Stop trying to fix the stronghold/addiction, struggle, character flaw, habit, action, behavior, emotion, or feeling without fixing the seed THOUGHT! What do you think about yourself? If that storyline is off, everything else will be out of alignment. Remember, whenever the initial thought is off, there is a domino effect for everything following the event. Stop and think HIGHER. Think higher of yourself. Think higher of others. Think higher about the

F. Y. I.

situation. Take your eagle's view and speak a new word. Edit the thought. Edit the seed and the fruit will align. Many of us make mistakes trying to keep thoughts from coming to our minds. We cannot control every thought that enters, but we can control which thoughts we will water and feed. If you want to renew your mind, you need to read the manufacturer's description of you. Ask the FATHER what HE says about you.

The following is a simple confessional I am learning to speak over myself:

I AM whole. I AM everything I was intended to be. I AM a portrait of beauty, physically and spiritually. I AM a gift to the universe, unique and necessary. I AM here to contribute something only I can offer. I AM confident that I am fearfully and wonderfully made. I AM not intimidated by any other creation. I AM not envious of anyone else's looks, life, or journey. I AM grateful for my own journey. I AM happy. I AM at peace. I AM fulfilled. I AM worthy of every good thing life has to offer me. I AM honored by every challenge I have the opportunity to overcome. I AM thankful for the life I live. I understand that breathing is evidence that my hopes and dreams still have a chance to come to pass. I AM becoming more of the person I was created to be each day. I truly love myself more than anyone else ever could.

I am so proud of you for reaching this point in the freedom journey. One more chapter to go. Take a moment to honor yourself for enduring this journey. Take a moment to acknowledge everything you've learned about yourself. Take a moment to think about your intention on this freedom journey. Recommit to achieving and sustaining them.

F. Y. I.

Chapter Ten

Free Indeed

Now that you are committed to walking in total liberty and victory in every area of your life, I would be less than honorable if I didn't provide you with tools to maintain this newfound freedom. Unfortunately, not everyone will be excited about your freedom. Sometimes, it's because they benefited from your imprisonment. Sometimes, they are not courageous enough to seek their own liberation and are angry with you for leaving them behind. Sometimes, they wanted to be your master. Sometimes, they don't know any better. There are a few great lessons you can provide for those people. The first is to get them a copy of this book to read for themselves. Additionally, here are some principles and tactics you can use to protect yourself from the temptation to go back into captivity.

1. Disarm
2. Disengage
3. Disable

We have covered so much getting to this place in the journey. You have learned how to identify your trigger points for each emotion you feel. You have learned how to trace the sequence of events back to the root. You have mastered the root-cause analysis of your life and have uprooted everything that was unprofitable for your success. You have declared freedom from both external and internal opinions that do not nurture or foster productivity. You have learned to drive your life. Everyone who drives understands that you are not always the only one on the road. Learning how to drive in an empty parking lot is one way. Learning to drive on a back road with no traffic is another way, but you are not considered a good driver until you have learned to drive with other traffic. Those of us who live in metropolitan areas understand even greater the need for defensive driving skills. Let's build your arsenal of defensive life driving.

Disarm

The first point we must do is disarm the obstacle. Identify the weapon and the intended emotion it is aimed for. By this point, we are no longer focused on the vehicle it's coming through. We can see past the person carrying it and focus on the sender. You don't get angry at the mail carrier for delivering the bill. You contact the person who sent the bill. Likewise, when you receive a comment or message from someone that has been a source of contention for you in the past, disarm the trigger point. You cannot disarm the sender. You simply control how you handle the message.

The only control I have in this world is self-control. It's the most powerful control there is.

ℱ. 𝒴. ℐ.

I want you to practice this every time it happens. When you receive a comment or message that hits an emotional button, be still. Then, I want you to listen to your thoughts concerning what you just heard or read. If you are reading it, you have time to decide whether or not you want to respond. In many cases, I would say do not respond. However, there are times when you should respond and how you respond will disarm the situation for you.

Therefore, if you read the message the first time, and it bothers you emotionally, stop. You have paid attention to your thoughts. Your thoughts are inviting some contrary emotions. Ok, wait! Hush your thoughts for a second. Go back and read the message again. Consider the source of the person who sent it. Are they someone who has been consistently positive or negative? If they are normally positive, consider what in it put you on the defense and see if it is valid. If it is not valid, then it's simple for you to redirect your original thought with the right perception of what you read. If you determine the message is sent with the intent to provoke a negative thought, emotion, or action from you there are a few responses I've trialed and found effective for me. I am an emotionally charged person, in the best and worst of ways. I can ruminate over a thought for hours and even days, which can completely derail my freedom train if I'm not careful. I've learned how to disarm an argument, tense conversation, or offensive comment.

- I'm sorry you are feeling this way. We have different takes on the situation. Have a better day.
- Let's discuss this at a later time when we are both open to understanding a broader perspective of the facts.
- Okay

F. Y. I.

That last one is my FAVORITE! It is the most confusing response for an adversarial spirit. I believe Solomon said, agree with a fool when he is in the way[34]. There is absolutely no need, wisdom, or consequential benefit to arguing when you know you are not going to find a resolution without reverting back to your old mentality. It is better to let them "win," so you can actually win by maintaining your peace, joy, and mental freedom from the unnecessary anguish foolishness attracts. A soft answer turns away wrath.[35] Solomon definitely said this.

If the intent is to make you angry, disarm the individual with a soft brief answer. If the intent is to embarrass you, disarm it with a statement of gratitude that the referenced part of your life is no longer your struggle. If the intent is to make you sad, disarm the situation with a statement of thankful reflection of your unspeakable joy. My mom would tell you, *"Don't feed into it."*

If you want to disarm a weapon, take away the ammunition.

A gun without a bullet cannot pierce through the flesh to internal access. A comment without your emotional trigger cannot produce an emotional response in or from you. Stop the thought that releases the emotion. You stop the thought by giving your brain a new thought to follow. Retell yourself the scenario in a way that teaches you a lesson and shifts your emotions back to gratitude.

I received a message on my phone this morning from someone who has struggled with celebrating my progress lately. It concerned my selection for promotion on my job. I opted not to notify this person of my great news because I

F. Y. I.

knew I would not get a happy response like everyone else. True to my point, their comment was as I expected. I had a choice to make. I could become angry and argue about why I didn't choose to notify this individual and justify my cause, or I could accept their emotional state for where it is and maintain my own state. Therefore, I chose the second option, and my response was "Thanks!" even though they weren't celebrating with me. Guess what happened next? The conversation ended!

One day, I will reach a place where I can send one-word responses to every negatively intended comment. I tend to type quite a bit, thinking I am really making people understand my point when in reality they are not trying to understand my point. Friend, save your breath, fingers, and emotions!

Disarm it: Okay, Thanks, Great, Interesting, BYE!

Disengage

Learn how to disengage before you are emotionally charged. One of the most common traps to lure you back into an emotional prison is causing you to grip something sinking. Every ship has an anchor. The purpose of the anchor is to keep the ship in place for an appointed time. The attendants on the ship lower the anchor, but they do not go down with the anchor. Whether in the middle of the sea or close to shore, the anchor is heavy enough to keep the ship or boat from drifting out of position.

In the event you do not effectively disarm the situation at the onset, you must intentionally disengage. If you are attempting to communicate, and it is not going well so that it is raising your blood pressure, tone, and volume, and your emotional switchboard is beginning to flash, end

F. Y. I.

the conversation! The best time to disengage is BEFORE you reach a designated emotion. My oldest sister, Davida, used to say this many times, and then, I began using the same phrase. She would say "You feel some type of way?" Now, I know she didn't make that up, but she's the first one I heard use it. Some type of way is a place where you are not quite sure what your emotions are about the situation. You're not sure if you're angry, sad, disappointed, or shocked. You know you are not feeling at ease, but not committed to an emotion yet. This is the place where you really need to disengage because once you settle into an emotion, you have to work to pull that anchor back up. Anchors are heavy!

When an emotional anchor is dropped in a relationship, all parties involved are stuck. If the emotion that lowered the anchor is negative that relationship will be stuck in a bad place until the anchor is fully disengaged. You never want to release an anchor in the middle of a relational storm. Disengage the unproductive communication. Sometimes, this will mean disengaging from any communication temporarily.

I have learned some practical ways to disengage. Silence the notifications if it is not a verbal conversation. If you are talking face to face, excuse yourself to a restroom. If you are speaking over the phone, excuse yourself to attend to something in front of you. Sometimes, even with disengaging from the communication, we are still actively engaged in the emotional rollercoaster attached to it. You must completely disengage from the argumentative thoughts that are racing through your mind. Remind yourself that you do not have to prove that you're right. Remind yourself that you do not have to win. Remind yourself that you do not have to get stuck in an emotional storm. You are capable of moving past this storm. You can

F. Y. I.

access the damage to the ship once you reach a peaceful place, not in the middle of the chaos. You are not the person you used to be and will not revert backward despite your desire to prove your point. Your new point is maintaining your freedom. Your new point is being free indeed! Your new point is being free indefinitely!

Disable

The third point is learning how to disable the trap for future use. Your job is to make this comment ineffective in the future. You must begin taking inventory of the phrases that cause the most temptation for you returning to a place of bondage. Once you identify the phrase, or song, or place that ensnares you, disable it.

I experienced a series of events that I logged as negative in a particular city. Every time I had to go to that city, pass through that city, or talk to people from that city, it was a trigger back to the prison I constructed for that place. However, I recently began thinking about the city a little more. I began taking inventory of everything I experienced while living there. I purchased my first home. I had two of my children there. I received a couple of promotions there. I released my first book there. I impacted many lives there. I met many beautiful people there.

A couple of weeks ago I was driving down with my brother Iric. I said to him in the car, "Man, this is the first time I'm going to this city, and I don't feel any anxiety, sadness, or apprehension about being seen or running into anyone." I actually made a point to visit a friend's church service. This is how I knew I was truly free from that stronghold. It wasn't just going there, but it was seeing people who used to be a trigger or connection to the prison.

F. Y. I.

I had absolutely nothing sparked in my heart that provoked anything other than love, joy, peace, excitement, and liberty. I disabled the weapon. That can no longer be used against me.

You have to find a way to disable the weapon. Completely destroy it! No place, no smell, no song, no movie scene, no comment should have the ability to torment or unsettle you repeatedly. The first time or two, you may not catch it. Nevertheless, once you realize the same weapon is getting you each time, you must take dominion and decide to face it directly with your head held high because you are free INDEED! Whatever it used to mean is something in the past, and now it is a monument of another place of victory!

YOUR RESPONSIBILITY

Once you have gone through your process of liberation and freedom, it is your responsibility to stay free. This means you must guard the company you keep. You must guard what you watch and listen to. You must maintain independent free thinking from the status quo of society. You are living according to a different standard of living. You will not view life the same way everyone else does. You will not respond to situations the same way everyone else does. You will not expect the same outcomes everyone else does. You are not concerned with how anyone else is thinking, feeling, or behaving. They are driving their own lives in their own lanes. You are driving your own life in your own lane. You have no need to share lanes.

You cannot blame anyone else for your thoughts, emotions, actions, habits, character, or life. You understand

𝓕. 𝒴. 𝐼.

the value of mastering your own mind. You are strategic in your thinking because you fight from a higher vantage point. You win every battle because your perspective is higher, broader, and clearer than it's ever been. When you have moments of doubt, fear, or insecurity simply return to a place of gratitude for the ability to identify, acknowledge, and address those old chains. You no longer are bound by the chains. You are at liberty to carry them and drop them at your leisure. You choose to carry them to GOD and drop them in prayer. You leave them there and return to your day with the assurance that all is truly well.

You are prepared and equipped to defend your liberty even from yourself. You will disarm every thought that rises in you that tells you anything contrary to your new identity. We can be our biggest problem because there are secrets we know about ourselves that no one else does. We know the thoughts that never turn into words or actions. Negative thoughts will come. You cannot control the initial thought that enters, but you can disarm every mental grenade before it detonates and causes damage. At the first contrary thought, stop, be still, pay attention to what you are saying to yourself and where it is coming from. Remind yourself that you deserve to live more abundantly. Everything in our lives starts with a thought that is either nurtured or disarmed, disengaged and disabled. The sooner you stop the progression of a toxic thought from turning into a toxic word, action, behavior, habit, etc., the better your stability will be.

The same tools you use to guard yourself against external weapons; you must use to guard yourself against internal weapons. Take the ammunition away from yourself. Once you have begun living with corrected vision, but when you remove your glasses off it becomes obvious how much you need to put them back on all the time. We

F. Y. I.

cannot control when life sends us a new lesson, challenge, or test. We must remain ready and alert at all times to disarm, disengage, and disable. I disarm myself by that I am not what I have done or experienced. I disengage from the downward thought cycles by telling myself, let it go. You couldn't change it when it happened. You cannot change it now. I disable my own weapons by reminding myself, that I am headed in an upward direction, and there is a weight limit on this journey. I'll just have to leave this issue where it is and keep marching forward.

I started using this prayer at the end of each day, and it has blessed me. You can pray this for yourself if you would like.

My Prayer for Me

GOD help me not to carry today's perspective of the situation into tomorrow. Help me not to rehearse a story to myself that is not 360 degrees of insight and accuracy. Help me not to make up the other person's thoughts, intentions, or feelings. And every hurtful memory, help me to process until it's reframed in a way that uplifts me and the other parties involved. LORD I thank you that YOU are sharpening my vision, understanding, and clarity each day. I yield every negative feeling I'm holding onto, whether for justification of my actions, degradation of the other person's character, or a means to keep me wounded and in need of rescue and support. Help me to be eager to stand in my capabilities and handle this situation with wisdom and insight. I thank YOU for trusting me to be an example even in this. May I forever tell the story YOU have written for my life. And in the moments my humanity supersedes my spirit, hide me in YOUR shadow until I am able to withstand the test. Thank you for developing good fruit in me and for giving me seed to sow into the lives of others.
AMEN

ℱ. 𝒴. ℐ.

My Prayer for You

GOD help my friends to find the courage to experience the abundant life YOU destined for them to live. Help them to understand their worthiness is secured in YOU. Help them to openly receive the abundance of YOUR love towards them. Fortify their courage to face their darkest secrets and come out victorious over every shameful, embarrassing, depressing, disheartening, and disqualifying memory. Give them 20/20 vision of their purpose and enlightenment on why every experience was/is necessary for their development. Grant them access to total liberty! Let them bask in it, so they will never settle for dysfunction again. Let them honor you in their journey and promised land. Let them shine like a beacon of light to those you've placed around them. Let their victory bring victory for everyone connected to them. LORD I thank YOU for allowing them to connect to YOUR purpose for my life. I am grateful for the chance to be a demonstrator. GOD, be just as great in their lives as YOU have been in mine, showing you are not a respecter of persons. And we will both give YOU the praise for YOUR mighty acts in our lives. AMEN.

Thank you so much for taking the time to read and apply the principles within this book. I pray that you feel empowered, equipped, and enabled to Free Yourself Indefinitely! The indefinite aspect comes with daily practice. It is not because there will never be a time when you will think or feel in ways that are captivating, but you are prepared to end each day in total liberty. In the beginning, every day will have many moments when you must consciously remember and apply what you've read. The great news is after you have actively applied these for

F. Y. I.

at least three weeks; this way of thinking becomes a habit. Once it is a habit, it will become a lifestyle, and that is how indefinite freedom becomes your portion.

I would love to hear from you. Let us know how this book reached you. I don't know what the future holds for you or me, but I know who holds the future, and I know we are well equipped for it all.

Many Blessings to you, Friend!

F. Y. I.

References

1. Genesis 3:8. *The Holy Bible*. King James Version.
2. Reiner, Rob, director. *A Few Good Men*. 1992
3. Exodus 3:1-4. *The Holy Bible*. King James Version.
4. Titus 3:5. *The Holy Bible*. King James Version.
5. Isaiah 46: 10. *The Holy Bible*. King James Version.
6. Jeremiah 29:11. *The Holy Bible*. King James Version.
7. Luke 14:11. *The Holy Bible*. King James Version.
8. Psalm 110:1. *The Holy Bible*. King James Version.
9. 1 Corinthians 13: 4-8. *The Holy Bible*. King James Version.
10. Proverbs 15:1. *The Holy Bible*. King James Version.
11. Provers 18:21. *The Holy Bible*. King James Version.
12. Genesis 1. *The Holy Bible*. King James Version.
13. 2 Corinthians 3:2-3. *The Holy Bible*. King James Version.
14. Matthew 5:39. *The Holy Bible*. King James Version.
15. Nehemiah 6:3. *The Holy Bible*. King James Version.
16. 1 Samuel 17: 34-37. *The Holy Bible*. King James Version.
17. 1 Corinthians 3:6-7. *The Holy Bible*. King James Version.

F. Y. I.

18. Mark 5:1-18. *The Holy Bible.* King James Version.

19. Psalm 30:5. *The Holy Bible.* King James Version.

20. Psalm119:71. *The Holy Bible.* King James Version.

21. Luke 22:42, Psalm 91:4. *The Holy Bible.* King James Version.

22. Matthew 14:30. *The Holy Bible.* King James Version.

23. Matthew 17:20. *The Holy Bible.* King James Version.

24. Matthew 24:21-23. *The Holy Bible.* King James Version.

25. 1 Peter 5:7. *The Holy Bible.* King James Version.

26. Matthew 11:29-30. *The Holy Bible.* King James Version.

27. Romans 4:18-22. *The Holy Bible.* King James Version.

28. Mark 9:23. *The Holy Bible.* King James Version.

29. Mississippi Children's Choir. "There is hope." 1992

30. Rocky Balboa, 2006, Sylvester Stallone

31. Merriam-Webster, 2019. Freedom. Retrieved from https://www.merriam-webster.com/dictionary/freedom

32. 2 Corinthians 4:7. *The Holy Bible.* King James Version.

33. Merriam-Webster, 2019. Perception. Retrieved from https://www.merriam-webster.com/dictionary/perception#other-words

F. Y. I.

34. Proverbs 26:4. *The Holy Bible.* King James Version.

35. Proverbs 15:1. *The Holy Bible.* King James Version.

Made in the USA
Lexington, KY
20 November 2019